Frederic Slater:
A Genius or Mischievous?

Book 1 – The Book Of Discoveries

THE OUT OF AUSTRALIA THEORY

By Steven and Evan Strong

With Frederic Slater

WARNING: To peoples of Australia (Ab)Original and Torres Strait Island descent this book contains the names and images of deceased people.

Published by Steven & Evan Strong, 2023, Australia

Website: https://forgottenorigin.com/
Conferences: https://www.ouralienancestry.net/
Email: stevenevanstrong@gmail.com
Phone: 61 0266281749
Facebook: https://www.facebook.com/Steven-and-Evan-Strong-198880073472926/
YouTube: https://www.youtube.com/c/Forgottenorigin

ISBN: - 978-0-9945268-2-3

ISBN (eBook): - 978-0-9945268-3-0

Copyright © Steven & Evan Strong
First edition, 2023

All rights reserved. No part of this publication may be reproduced, stored in a retrieval system or transmitted in any form by any means, electronic, mechanical, by photocopy or otherwise, without the prior writer permission of the publisher and copyright holders.

Author: Steven & Evan Strong
Title: Frederic Slater: Genius or Mischievous?

Subjects: history/ cultural studies/ archaeology/ anthropology/ geology/ genetics/ comparative religious studies/ mythology/spirituality/ human origins

Also, by Steven & Evan Strong:
Between a Rock and a Hard Place
Out of Australia
Forgotten Origin
Mary Magdalene's Dreaming: a Comparison of Aboriginal wisdom & Gnostic Scriptures
Constructing a New World Map

Also, by Steven Strong & Lea Kapiteli:
Interview with an Alien

Typesetting and design: Erica Schmerbeck
Printed by: Ingram Spark

For The Reader:

- WARNING: To peoples of Australia (Ab)Original and Torres Strait Island descent this book contains the names and images of deceased people
- The word Aboriginal / (Ab)Original is replaced with the word Original to describe the Indigenous Peoples of Australia.
- Surnames of deceased Australia Original Elders, Custodians and peoples are with-held to observe protocols of respect and culture.
- Other names have been changed/With-held to ensure the security and safety of some of our sources.

Dedication:

To Frederic Slater: a gentleman scholar, journalist, researcher, historian, writer, editor, and an intellectual anarchist.

Your bravery and legacy lives on.

We are hoping this book assists in rectifying the import of your works and your position as a seminal researcher of Australian & world history, religion/spirituality, language, and esoteric philosophy.

You paved the way for the rest of us to follow thank you.

Figure 1: Frederic Slater's Grave Marker[1]

Acknowledgements

Forward by **Paul Wallis.**

Introduction, 1, 2, 3, 5, 7, 9, 11, 12 & 13 by **Steven & Evan Strong**.

Chapters 4, 6, 8, 10 by **Frederic Slater.**

Chapter 14 by Roy Goddard (Included in Slater's "Scribes of the Stone Age" original manuscript).

Appendix 1

"Discovery of Australia by de Quiros in the Year 1606" by Cardinal Patrick Moran.

Appendix 2:

"Burragurru or Devil's Rock: an aboriginal burial ground in the Wollombi district" by Roy Goddard.

Appendix 3:

"Jon Wyatt's Email to Steven on Slater's The Newspapers" by Jon Wyatt.

Jon Wyatt for extensive research and opening the motherload of research on Slater. This book would not be in existence without you.

Erik Bower for his extensive research and pictures **(Figures 1 & 34).**

Paul Wallis for the excellent forward.

Samarah Wood for pictures **(Figures 30, 31 & 55).**

Ildi Budai for picture **(Figure 28).**

Gavin Bragg & Alan Gresley for picture **(Figure 29).**

Geraldine Grace for legal advice.

Contents

Foreword
By Paul Wallis: **8**

Introduction: 10

Chapter 1
Hidden and Lost in a Forgotten Filing Cabinet   12

Chapter 2
Frederic Slater's Scribes Of The Stone Age   16

Chapter 3
The Inconvenient Truths   24

Chapter 4
"The Pharaohs of the South Land" by Frederic Slater   33

Chapter 5
Civilised Behaviour   37

Chapter 6
"Words on the Rocks" by Frederic Slater   42

Chapter 7
Wollombi and Gosford: Home Base   44

Chapter 8
"Symbolic Writing" by Frederic Slater   56

Chapter 9
The Date Would be Nearer to 100,000 years   60

Chapter 10
"Stone Age Authors" by Frederic Slater   74

Chapter 11
The Hows, Whys, Who and Where   78

Chapter 12
Finding Nemo   84

Chapter 13
Nobody Cared   87

Chapter 14
Goddard's Report by Roy Goddard   90

Appendix 1
"Discovery of Australia by de Quiros in the Year 1606" By Patrick F. Cardinal Moran, Archbishop of Sydney   93

Appendix 2
Goddard's Section within Chapter 6 "Words on the Rocks" by Roy Goddard   119

Appendix 3
Jon Wyatt's Email to Steven on Slater's "The Newspapers"   128

Other Books: 130

About the Authors: 140

Bibliography: 141

Endnotes:
References & Notes: 147

Index   163

Foreword

BY PAUL WALLIS:

Author of the bestselling trilogy: Escaping from Eden, The Scars of Eden and Echoes of Eden.

Frederic Slater is a name which deserves to be known by every student of anthropology, linguistics, or archaeology - and indeed by anyone with an interest in human origins and the pre-history of Australia. The story of Frederic Slater's research into these fascinating fields offers us an object lesson in a tendency within academia to limit rather than expand our exploration of vital questions.

The Greek philosopher-scientist, Plato, honored for two and half millennia as one of humanity's greatest minds, wrote about a body of information bequeathed to history by the Greek legislator Solon. Solon had gleaned this information from the remnant of the priestly caste of Egypt. In turn these Egyptian priests claimed that their information about our planet and its prehistoric populations was sourced from the remnant of an even more ancient civilization – a global civilization whose genius was even more advanced than that of pre-dynastic Egypt.

Yet all this time later, it is almost a taboo to suggest that, prior to the cataclysm of the most recent ice age, which so nearly rendered homo sapiens extinct, there existed a civilization which grew and spread to span the globe. Rather than probe this intriguing possibility, the picture we have preferred is of primitive man emerging from his ancestral primate family and then gradually upgrading in intelligence and sophistication until eventually he became us! As a young student of languages and linguistics I vividly remember raising an eyebrow or two when I first learned that the history of the world's languages appears to contradict this preferred consensus. Rather the deep history of languages and their development would appear to point the arrow in entirely the opposite direction, hinting at a human past that was more sophisticated than today; more intelligent, more ordered, and more harmonious. But how could that possibly be?

We can be grateful to publishers and collaborators prior to the Second World War for having shone a light on the anthropological work of Frederic Slater, who at that time was already known and respected as a journalist and editor of four newspapers. This side of the war, Slater's far-reaching conclusions were to suffer, not for lack of credibility or corroboration, but for convincingly pointing in a direction opposite to that of the mainstream consensus, which espoused the gradual evolution of humanity from colonies of animal-skin-wearing savages in Africa to the apex of modern Western Civilization.

Slater's works were inconvenient not only to academic paleontologists and anthropologists but to the powers of empire – and specifically to the claim of the British royal family as the rightful owners of the Australian continent. Slater's highlighting of Catholic Spain's prior claim, and his affirmation of the cultures already present in Australia, estimating their antiquity at more than 150,000 years, pitched him decisively against the political establishment of British Australia.

This was the course which ensured that Slater's contribution to world knowledge would be progressively ridiculed and airbrushed from history.

And that is where the story of Frederic Slater's contribution to world thought might have ended were it not for an abandoned filing cabinet and the tireless work of Steven and Evan Strong, whose research, tenacity and courage have resulted in the important book you are now holding. As you journey through its pages, the bones and skulls of Australian hominids, archeological artefacts, stone carvings, rock paintings, standing stones and the Dreaming of Australia's original peoples will begin to open up before you and reveal their great secrets.

To make this journey in the company of Steven and Evan Strong is a profound pleasure. Their intimate connection with the original peoples of Australia allows us to draw from wells which are tens of thousands of years deep. Yet in the company of traditional elders and guardians this great expanse of time is brought palpably into the present.

In this book, Steven and Evan offer the world a great gift in unearthing this story, which they tell in a compelling and evocative style, which will draw you ever deeper into the odyssey of discovery and drama of Frederic Slater's incredible career. What that odyssey offers includes the secrets of ancient Aboriginal language, vocabulary, glyphs, pictograms, ideograms, and literature. All of these carry a cultural memory of humanity's deep past, and our great leap forward in agriculture and civil engineering. Similarly, the mysteries of Australian caves, rock formations, standing stones and prehistoric ceremony, reveal an ancestral memory of our forebears' first contact with visitors from the stars. In short, you will find that a veritable library of original Australian knowledge offers to transform our whole understanding of ourselves as species and our place in the cosmos.

The information in the pages that follow is powerful and persuasive, logical and scholarly. Be ready for your assumptions to be challenged and for the ground of long held paradigms to shift under your feet as you read. Turn the page and continue to the end, and I predict that you will be astonished and enriched by that journey.

Now is a time of remembering. Together we are learning to give a respectful hearing to places and voices our parents and grandparents were taught to dismiss and disparage. Now is the perfect time to rediscover Fredric Slater, to rediscover prehistoric Australia, and open ourselves to the deep and rich knowledge of its ancient land and original peoples. In the company of my courageous friends, Steven and Evan Strong, let us make the journey together.

Paul Wallis
Ngambri and Ngunnuwal Country
November 2022

Introduction:

This is the first instalment, there will be no less than four more to follow. The reason why we are compelled to break up Frederic Slater's book[1], Scribes of the Stone Age[2], into sections is simply because it is so radical, unique and incredibly profound in rewriting virtually all of Australia's pre-history, and there is a need to move slowly so as to pause, reflect and absorb in 'bite-sized' segments. He begins this journey into the ancient past by insisting that the Great Record Book he was given can interpret not only the meanings of all ancient stone engravings of Australia, but can do the same anywhere on this planet.

The content in this recently recovered manuscript, of which the edited book was assumed to be destroyed while awaiting publication in London during the German blitzkrieg in World War 2, has so many lost secrets, extensions and surprises. Slater stated on many occasions that humanity reached its peak at the very beginning, and since that auspicious start, it has been a continuous downhill slide. He cites passages on the rocks that speak of coming to Earth with seven senses fully developed. From that sensational starting point, it gets even more intriguing in that the very first language spoken throughout the planet and recorded on rock is also called Soul Language. The icing on this 'esoteric cake' is all about these Sky Heroes[3] who travelled from distant constellations and not only came to this planet, but were heavily involved in human genetics, evolution, history and the oncoming change in the global transformation of everything.

In the first of at least five books, our contribution is greater than Slaters, we have no choice. In setting the scene and cleaning up the collateral damage concocted by the 'experts,' we have provided commentaries, elaborations and some empirical proof validating what Slater raised in the first four chapters and an archaeological paper he co-wrote. We were forced to devote two chapters delving into Slater's past and impeccable reputation, as there have been so many unwarranted critiques and aspersions relating to Slater's integrity, intentions and mental health. What immediately stands out in this sea of negativity, is that all the critics cannot supply one quote or word cited from Slater's work. His archaeological book was assumed lost, his personal letters (of which we have) have never been examined and they falsely claimed he never wrote a scientific paper. All of these many criticisms and distractions are utterly unjustified and require a thorough rebuttal before beginning any analysis of this seminal book, and the amazing content within.

Amongst all the brilliant and insightful interpretations and observations Slater chronicled in the 1930's when dating analysis and archaeology was still in its infancy, there are two understandable minor errors he did make that needs to be cleared up before beginning this report. First up, knowing that Original[4] mathematics never spanned into hundreds of thousands, it needs to be appreciated that Slater supplied a variety of figures in relation to when Original culture was established. He does provide a marked contradiction in offering one hundred thousand all the way through to three hundred thousand years. At no stage does he claim these numbers were found engraved on the rocks, and granted does equivocate in adding at least, but we are convinced the number is far greater. In fact, we feel Original people originated in Australia, and never came to Australia from anywhere.

And that brings us to the second mistake in Slater's book. He often states that the Original people of Australia came from Egypt way back. The Egypt he envisages being so advanced so long ago and whatever number he provides, never existed. Going past ten thousand is not even feasible, throwing extra noughts on top just doesn't apply. Nor is there any record on the rocks explicitly stating this locality, however, we can see why Slater did select Egypt. He knew there was a culture of high sophistication involved, but not so that Egypt is a much more modern rebound of Atlantis, nor was he aware that Australia was a part of Lemuria. Such knowledge and theories were rarely discussed when Slater put his book together. From his perspective before Egypt everything else was less refined and esoteric.

Those minor errors aside, everything else is as it was so long ago.

It all comes down to one imperative, if Slater's interpretations sourced from the Great Record Book are indeed correct, then literally everything written and assumed to be fact when discussing humanities ancient past is wrong on almost every count.

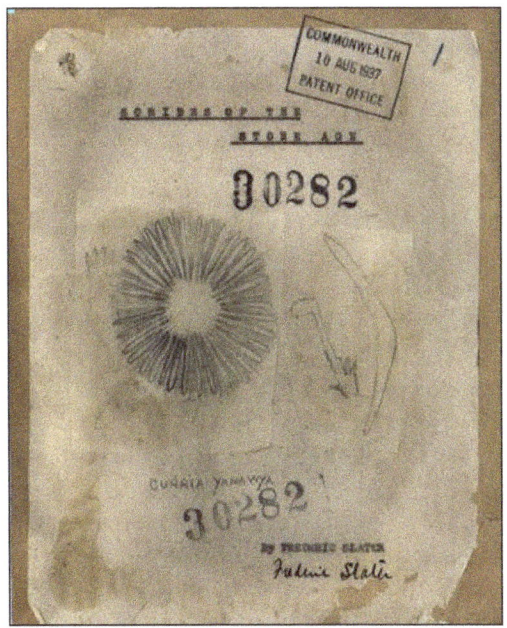

Figure 2: Cover Image of Slater's Scribes of the Stone Age[5]

Chapter 1

HIDDEN AND LOST IN A FORGOTTEN FILING CABINET

Richard Patterson had just joined the Mullumbimby branch of the Historical Society, and when standing in the back room a filing cabinet that was quite old caught his attention. There was nothing special or impressive about this discarded cabinet and it certainly served no current purpose beyond taking up room. Once finding the key he opened the cabinet and inside was a large cardboard box, clearly very old and without a label or writing detailing the contents.

There inside was a hand-drawn map of 184 Standing Stones and eighteen handwritten letters[1] penned by a person whose name was Frederic Slater, which meant nothing to Richard. All of these letters were addressed to someone who was local, in fact he was, before World War 2, the local headmaster of the Brunswick Heads primary school. His name was Fred Fordham. Apart from sharing the same first name with a minor variation in spelling, nothing else registered on Richard's radar.

That all changed once Richard began to read what Slater had written. The content was a series of directions, observations, explanations, and elaborations regarding a sacred site of phenomenal dimensions, rock tonnage and many constructions. Numbering over one-hundred rock arrangements, some containing hundreds of rocks of which quite a few weighed tonnes, there was one central site of 184 Standing Stones which stood out. The design, height of some monoliths that stood upright several metres in height, and accompanying interpretations of what they meant, broke every rule and rewrote fundamental elements of not only Australian, but world pre-history.

There was talk of ancient Egyptians sailing to this sacred complex, of Sky Heroes from the stars arriving and sharing everything from philosophy through to genetics, that the Australian Original people were the keepers of the most civilised society and knowledge ever known and a constant stream of comparisons to other ancient societies. Literally everything began in Australia, well that is how this person saw things, but as for absolute proof, there was some in the letters and references to one book which was called Scribes of the Stone Age, but because he made so many sensational claims and interpretations, more was needed.

Soon after reading some of his letters Richard approached Evan and I and made copies of everything in the filing cabinet and gave them to us. Not long after I was talking to the person who openly admitted being responsible for the destruction of the entire complex of which there were tens of thousands of rocks. And so this journey into the real history and legacy of the Original people of long ago began with this first step. After close to a dozen conversations, the 91-year-old farmer gave me permission to do two days of archaeology on the mound upon which the 184 stones were either bulldozed down the steep slope, or if too large and heavy, taken individually to the dairy and stacked in five rows.

The one consistency this man had during our discussions was a genuine remorse and sincere regret for what he did when obeying his father's directive. There were times when tears were running down his cheeks as we talked. We do not intend to present arguments for and against its legitimacy now, as we actually devoted seven chapters establishing the authenticity of the Standing Stones Complex in an earlier book of ours called Between a Rock and a Hard Place. However, we feel there is one very special event orchestrated by my Boss Elder, Ramindjeri[2] Elder Karno W., that not only validates the site but equally brings back this sacred, and what Slater would deem to be civilised, heritage and wisdom which inspired and maintains the site he called Australia's Stone Henge.

Figure 3: Between a Rock and a Hard Place[3]

Karno Calling

Once I had permission for a two-day examination of the mound and surrounds, our first and overriding priority was to arrange for Karno to come and supervise the mystical side of this research. Without him being there orchestrating proceedings, there would be no-one else versed in Old Way protocol and nothing of esoteric substance would eventuate. He did come and after quite a few meetings with local Elders it was agreed by all that even though his tribal estate was thousands of kilometres to the south-west, he would be in charge once we began.

I still remember after we had met with the farmer who checked the personnel present, he made it very clear no member of any Lands Council was to be part of this archaeological field work, everyone assembled assumed we were about to start. We had twenty odd volunteers in the team who came from all over the country, and ten local Elders plus Karno, and once the farmer had given permission, I spoke to those gathered. I could tell from the sighs, quizzical looks and slumped shoulders what I said was not well received. I made it clear admission had to be granted twice over, once from the farmer and secondly from the resident guardian Spirits of the site, and if they replied in the negative, we must all pack up and leave.

Figure 4: Standing Stones Site[4]

Myself and ten Elders, plus Karno, left the group and made our way along a dirt track towards the mound that once housed the 184 Standing Stones. Karno and another Elder, Jarmbi'je, were calling out to the "Old Ones"[5] as we got closer. Many of the group followed Karno as he made his way to where the southern circle of rocks once stood. It wasn't long after before he broke into song, an Old Way First Language song presumably asking the Spirits for a rite of passage. And it didn't take long before they first appeared circling above Karno.

Figure 5: Hawk[6]

There were hawks flying directly above, two that circled him. He kept singing as two was nowhere near enough. Soon after three more hawks answered his call, and now there were five hawks circling Karno and his song. But from Karno's perspective the song was not finished and nor was the circle, shape or numbers desired. Three more came, which totalled eight but with one difference, the geometry had transformed into a figure-eight and Karno was smiling. The Spirits had agreed, and we could now begin our two-day investigation.

I still vividly remember what happened next and to this day it still doesn't make sense if living in the material world. Karno told me permission has been granted and to tell the others they can come, and in doing so, I was to follow the shadow of the hawk and make sure "you keep up."[7] Easier said than done, there was a hawk-shadow on the dirt track, and all the way back, while running at my top speed, that shadow remained on the track just in front. I remember wondering how is it that the shadow stayed so truly aligned to the path, and what was just as odd is how did it maintain such a dawdling pace? What I never did was look up, but if I had, I doubt there would have been feathers in flight directly above, but something far more ethereal in body and soul.

Figure 6: Karno W.[8]

When I did get back to the others, I was absolutely sure we had the right to investigate and honour this very special sacred Complex. Slater was correct in his interpretations at this site, and if that was the case here, it must be so everywhere. What follows in this first instalment is not so much the empirical proof, that comes later, but more an overview of what these engravings on rock meant in the past, and will mean again in days not far off.

Chapter 2

FREDERIC SLATER'S SCRIBES OF THE STONE AGE

In the simplest terms it has to be one or the other. It comes down to this, either Slater is the greatest Australian archaeologist of the twentieth century or the greatest liar and con man. Many experts have stated he is merely a charlatan at best and more likely deluded and clinically mad. They pay no account to his work or interpretations, but in doing so break one cardinal academic rule. In every critique there is not one syllable quoted from any of Slater's papers or book, none have seen his eighteen letters, in fact this academic's work has been supposedly lost for over eighty years. That being an incontestable truth until a month ago, how could anyone pass a positive or negative judgement if no evidence is presented? That approach is universally accepted to be bad science, and should be consigned to the rubbish bin.

In what only adds to the intrigue and multiplies the contradictions is that of the dozens of articles in the press throughout the 1930's mentioning Slater and his research, there is not one solitary word offered in doubt, ridicule or criticism. Not one of his colleagues are quoted anywhere in contesting Slater, in fact, until we came upon his notes and the news of the 184 Standing Stones he was analysing, no-one knew who he was nor of his research. Not one current academic knew of the existence of any paper, report or book, but nevertheless, with nothing to directly reference critiques were quickly cobbled together. If a Slater timeline was compiled it would be broken into three sections, pre–World War 2 is all complimentary, after the war until the Standing Stone site was rediscovered, there is a totally constructed vacuum, and since then he has transformed into a mischievous, somewhat deranged charlatan.

But now, with all his written work, which totals over one thousand pages, being sent to us, the other side of this Original equation is available to accept or refute. Now with his writings and research recovered, along with the semantics and structure of the First Language ever spoken on this planet, we can finally pass a judgement as to whether Frederic Slater is indeed a genius as we believe, or merely a mischievous rogue as many allege.

The Critic's Hit List

The opening gambit in all dismissals of Slater's credibility and integrity begin with concerns of his erratic verging on mad character. His family were approached recently, and the feedback was disparaging in his eccentricity, but equally, they stressed he did know a lot about the Original people and their culture. Nevertheless, what dominated the reports on his integrity was that he was someone who was more than a touch loopy. At worst even if this 'mad scientist' stereotype is fitting, of itself, this has no bearing on the truthfulness of the person under scrutiny.

What also needs to be considered in any attempt to determine the truthfulness and capacities of a person none met, is that how many experts before World War 2 were talking about Sky Heroes coming from space that were not born of the earth, how many were so openly empathetic and in awe of Original history and were insistent that ancient Egyptians came to Australia in a sacred pilgrimage? The answer is none, and anyone who did hold to these beliefs would certainly be ridiculed by those close to him as being odd and radical. Traits like these are never fostered during times of war and the immediate grief that follows.

The second condemnation on the list of Slater's faux paus is that yes, he was the President of the Australian Archaeological Educational and Research Society, but it had barely a dozen members and therefore, is of no consequence and can be summarily dismissed. By who? At that time there was not one faculty of archaeology or anthropology in any Australian University, the very first faculty to study anthropology under the direction Professor Elkin[1] began at Sydney University in 1939. Before that nearly all Australian archaeology was volunteer, almost always by highly educated members, but as for actual Australian home-grown and qualified archaeologists, there were none. That being the empty truth, to get double figures in a Sydney meeting is a good roll up as I doubt within the entire population at that time those with such skills and passion would never number past three figures.

Next up, Slater had no credibility, he wrote no paper and had no support or standing amongst his colleagues. In summation, these omissions is the base line of a feature article appearing in the Queensland leading newspaper, *The Courier Mail*. In refuting the authenticity of Slater's investigation into the Standing Stones, they posted a photograph of a person who does look somewhat unconventional in appearance with flaring eyes and a wide thin waxed moustache, and is named by the paper to be Frederic Slater. The problem is that it just isn't him, the sceptical academics who interviewed the family were given a photo of Slater which they have used many times since. But the inconvenient truth is that he looks so conservative and conventional in dress and presence, so a touch of poetic license was used by the paper to strengthen their denials, but alas this is not the only example of outright misleading fabrication.

Figure 7: Frederic Slater - The Wrong Person/Photograph[2]

We have a copy of the very important paper on a highly significant site called Burragurra, and it is co-authored by Slater and a highly respected academic, whose photograph is found in the halls of Sydney University. It was published in 1938 and we have numerous press clippings of this paper having been read out and "I am pleased with the publicity that has been given to the paper"[3] at the 1938 Australian and New Zealand Science Conference. So, we then knew of one paper, now we know of many more that have come our way, and that means it is not only the photo that is incorrect and badly researched, so too is their false claim he never wrote a scientific paper.

As for the implication he had no support or publicity, that is again manifestly untrue, in fact, of the dozens of press clippings we have found via Erik Bower's diligence in trawling through micro-fiche press of pre-World-War 2, not one critical or even doubting word is printed. Half of page 6 in the premiere Adelaide daily paper has Slater referring to his acquired manual of the First Language spoken on the planet, of Egyptians coming to Australia as learners and students, and so he continues[4]. But throughout this excerpt and all others never is an alternative expert with a contradicting viewpoint interviewed or cited. It is always the same, whether the Standing Stones site or one of his many other activities, his work was both worthy of publication and always above criticism.

What also can be easily compiled is the large number of highly educated volunteers who gave their time, energy and assistance when Slater was on site or in research. If he was as demented and irrational as present-day critiques allege, why is it so many intelligent academics and professional men willingly worked alongside, were publicly associated with him and allowed him to name them as part of his team? I suppose it is possible they are just as unhinged, but their elevated standing and the continued respect they received suggests the opposite.

Figure 8: Burragurra[5]

Freedom of the Press, but Which one?

In concluding Slater's background check and review of the condemnation by many academics and *The Courier Mail*, we believe what was reported in the free press when Slater was alive, in particular a section with quotation marks attributed to him, is not only the final word, but the truth as it was then and still is now.

"As translator of the Aboriginal writings on the rocks, as revealed in the colossal picturegrams at the Wollombi. I am pleased with the publicity that has been given to the paper read before the Science Congress. I think, however, that due credit is due to the explorers who did the field work and discovered them and sent the drawings to me to elucidate. It is more than a year ago that the first of the picturegrams was discovered by a party led by Mr. W. J. Enright, solicitor, of Maitland, former President of the Anthropological Society of Sydney, and well known for his work in collaboration with other scientists. With him was Mr. Roy H. Goddard, chartered accountant, an authority on Australian Aboriginal artifacts, who did the drawings from which the translations have been made. Mr. Goddard is one of the delegates of the Sydney Anthropological Society at the Science Congress. The other member of the party was Mr. Carlyle Greenwell, an architect of Sydney, who is at present in London.

I submit that the work of these explorers-archaeologists is the proper word-has brought to light confirmation of the origin of our native race ... and that our natives are survivors of the original race."[6]

When it comes to the 184 Standing Stones, plus the thousands of stones that made up the other stone monuments nearby, once again it was another person of high social and professional standing who compiled photographs, drawings and relevant information. And as before with other associates, his vocation affords a high degree of authority, as Mr. Fordham was the Principal of the Brunswick Valley Primary School. He spent over a year using up every available non-teaching moment on the site. In combination, Slater only worked with men from the highest levels of mainstream society, and this proves once again how tenuous and incorrect these later-day denials and alleged character deficiencies are.

Then The Walls and Standing Stones Came Tumbling Down

The selected press clipping above is dated January 15, 1939, but by the end of that year a World War had begun, and Slater's reputation was in tatters. He was shunned by all academic and political circles and all that he had done and interpreted was destroyed, hidden or forgotten.

That same Wollombi[7] paper that was so well received in 1937 was "CANCELLED"[8] by the Department of Public and Tropical Medicine, based at Sydney University, on the 8th of December 1938. One could ask, what expertise in Australian archaeology resides within a faculty that specialises in medicine, and the answer would be at best marginal and most likely much less. Nevertheless, the paper has a dated disclaimer of "cancelled"[9] stamped on the front page.

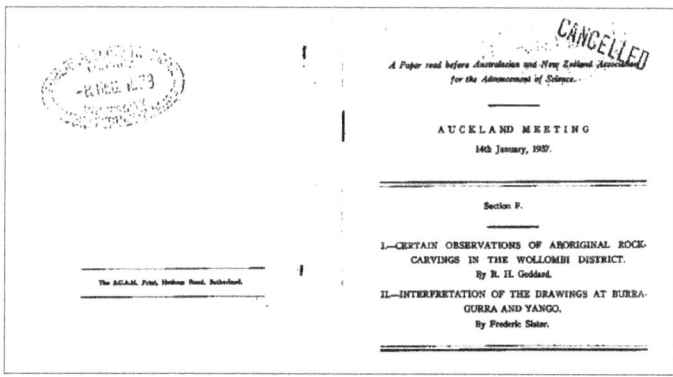

Figure 9: The Cancelled Paper[10]

It becomes increasing clear when reading his hand-written instructions and comments addressed to Fordham, that those in control are turning on Slater and in particular the site he was so focussed upon. Slater was very concerned that not only had the Government authorities threatened the owners of the farm by letter, but they had also personally visited the farm owner. So outraged was Slater by the devious nature of this intervention he reminded Fordham not to trust anyone who represented the Australian Museum or Sydney University, and stated he would personally contact and remonstrate those government appointed officials who came to the farmer's door.

Further on in his correspondence his mood becomes more sombre, and he changes tact knowing those in control are conspiring against him and this sacred site. In response he takes the pro-active step of contacting the Carnegie Institute seeking funding and gravitas. This initial enquiry bears positive fruit, then the war begins, and that positive path/solution evaporates. Not long after the farmer relents under the pressure and threats of eviction and tells his 15-year-old son (who I met and spoke to often before he gave me permission to do archaeology for two days) to start up the tractor and destroy the site. Whether by coincidence or government incentives, that same farm which had a sizeable mortgage held by the CBC Bank as the war began, is fully repaid by the farmer and in his possession months after the site was destroyed.

A Reality Check

Slater was not mad nor blighted with any psychological disorder. He was respected and assisted by many of his peers, he did write quite a few archaeological papers and liaised with people of high character and intelligence. Most importantly, he had in his possession a First Language reference manual compiled by Eliza Dunlop[11] in 1830. She was the wife of the first magistrate at Wollombi and won the trust of the local tribal leader who shared with her the words, symbols and picturegrams that make up the very first language spoken on the planet. Slater was given this extremely important document by his colleague Goddard[12], who is the grandson of Dunlop and understandably did not want to step so far outside the academia perimeter fences, while Slater was more adventurous and bolder.

Figure 10: Eliza Hamilton Dunlop[13]

We had assumed all his work was sent to his London publisher in 1939 and the publishing house was bombed with his work destroyed. But no, a second copy of his book, Scribes of the Stone Age, plus all of his papers remained in this country hidden for so long. The drawback when in denial and hiding the truth is that it can only be a short-term project, and they are now back to state their case. However, before beginning any analysis of the credibility of Slater's interpretations, we had to first clear away the obstacles and distortions. With the coast partially cleared, it is time to introduce snippets of Slater's research into ancient original Lore and pre-history.

An Aperitif

This selection of quotes is taken from the first introductory chapter and provides parameters and some sensational settings that sit well outside the reach of all accepted historical accounts. At the most basic level we are told by the experts that humanity began its ascension on the bottom rung, grunting and dribbling, then inching upwards and step by step we became more civilised and intelligent. Not according to Slater, in fact, he reverses the process so much so that pinnacle upon which the human journey began has never been emulated since.

From Slater's perspective "man in the beginning of time had a higher sense of his duty to man and the development of life-which to him was the soul-than can be found in the cultured nations of 2,000 years ago or the nations of today."[14] He is adamant that "there never has been a time since mankind came into the world that civilisation had not a place in his philosophy of life."[15]

And how could Slater know of such controversial historical truths, it is simply because "primordial man could write"[16] and in Australia this took place through what he called "picture language."[17] Unfortunately, the engravings and paintings in Australia "have been the despair of anthropologists and archaeologists. All know they are records, but the method of deciphering they failed to discover."[18] Through the access he was given to Dunlop's records of the First Language he was able to "open the picture book,"[19] and be able to correctly read and understand the "picture language of an ancient people."[20] And as an added bonus, Slater was willing to share this arcane wisdom as "the key will be found in these pages."[21]

Figure 11: The Key[22]

Make no mistake this is not just the source of language and writing Slater is dealing with, but includes all elements that make up this concept of "civilisation"[23] Slater often refers to. He believes that it was in Australia that the first "base of religion"[24] originated. "Their simple faith-they knew the Light of Heaven as the Soul of the Earth-was the foundation of the Egyptian Book of the Dead, the philosophy of Kon-fu-tse of China, the religion of the Akkadians…"[25]

The mainstream version of human habitation in Australia is locked into beginning 50-60,000 years ago. Slater would stridently object and multiply by a factor of no less than three. His book, "The Scribes of the Stone Age, carries the world's history back 150,000 years at least." [26] All of these observations given by Slater are not personal musings or predictions but based solely upon what he interpreted when examining these "picturegrams"[27] and symbols. Because he actually had "the method of deciphering"[28] in the book he was given. To find the correct meaning was simply a matter of compare, contrast and match.

Twenty Pages in and Over Six Hundred to go

This is meant to be the first part of an opening gambit. Primarily my aim in this initial report on Slater's written research was to clean up the drama, distractions and critiques, then give a very small sampling of what Slater had interpreted. Somewhere further on in his book is the "key"[29] that can unlock the wisdom of the ages. As Slater stated, "archaeologists have little idea of the wealth of records awaiting the investigator in Australia."[30] But if you do have the key to unlock these precious secrets, we have no doubt that many more new and ancient ideas will start to bubble to the surface.

It comes down to one of two alternatives; this man is either a genius well ahead of his time or is downright mischievous and culturally corrupt. The only way to decide is to read his work first, then pass judgement, and so far, not one critic or detractor has done this. What that means is he could be right in some or all of what he claims, and knowing that all accounts about Eliza Dunlop concede she was a writer of Original songs and language, that she did win the trust and respect of the local tribe in very early settler days, it is quite possible Slater was in possession of her work and is a genius.

Figure 12: To Hand Over[31]

As to whether the rest of the content in this book provides the standard of proof required, well this manuscript was accepted for publication in London. The editors and academics who read his manuscript would clearly recognise the sensational nature of his claims, that they agreed to publish indicates and they were satisfied with the rigour of argument and convincing evidence assembled.

We will be sharing much more, but with discretion, particularly when dealing with sensitive issues relating to First Language, as some fundamental base-words are very sacred, powerful and should only be vocalised during ceremony or rituals. What I do know through reading his eighteen letters and one remaining archaeological paper is that up ahead in those six hundred plus pages there will be mention a plenty of Egyptians in Australia seeking spiritual and magical tuition (the next chapter is called *Pharaohs of the Southern Land),* Aliens not born from this planet landing and sharing and that Australian Originals are the first race and literally everything written about pre-Cook Australia is wrong.

Beyond that we suspect there will so much more wisdom and reversals in his book and papers, and the chances are high it will be so, so needed in these deceitful fearful days, where the truth is taking such a shameful battering.

Chapter 3

THE INCONVENIENT TRUTHS

The overriding reality is that all of this comes down to determining if Frederic Slater is a man who is honest in character, and whether his claim that he is able to interpret stone-age picturegrams found all over the planet is actually true. If he is telling the truth then his written reports, in particular his major work Scribes of the Stone Age, changes literally everything we know about our evolution, history and reason for existing. If he is lying, as many recent critics insist, he is a rogue and shameful liar.

The fundamental problem is that all recent condemnations have nothing to do with what he actually wrote and everything to do with who he supposedly is. It has been claimed by present-day critics that Frederic Slater is "NOT an academic"[1] nor is he a "scholar"[2] and he was "NOT widely recognised."[3] In what only confirmed his lack of credibility and devious intentions was that his "family doesn't take anything he's done in archaeology (or many other areas) seriously AT ALL."[4] We cannot be certain as to whether his entire family communally yelled the words "AT ALL,"[5] or the author added the capital letters as a crude literary device. Regardless, through a combination of denigration and disdain, the inference is that 'All' his written work, although totally unknown and unseen, is false and no more than a serialised journey into pure fantasy and deceitful fabrication.

What we do find as fascinating as it is contradictory is the second half of Richard Slater's critique of his ancestor, while expressing "concerns about Slater's credibility"[6] he also openly admitted that "I am confident that he knew an awful lot about Indigenous people, including their myths."[7] And it is at this juncture there is a need to pause and reflect upon the first actual mention of the content and research he undertook. To begin by insisting "he knew an awful lot"[8] is by any academic standard a recommendation that stands above everything else. Whether or not he is widely known and a scholar, as is the case with the amateur who discovered the 'mythical' remains of Troy, has no relevance in deciding the authenticity of any archaeology. What is undeniably true is that many great scientists of the past were often beset by insecurities, were lacking social graces and regarded as being awkward or even loopy. That is an incontestable historical scientific fact, but as to whether Slater had similar personal failings, we believe that allegation is clearly not true, it is no more than a carefully constructed lie of convenience through censorship. The underlying intention is simple, by sullying his character it inevitably taints all of his research, papers and books, and by association, the sacred sites and incredibly ancient wisdom he translated all becomes collateral damage.

What we now know to be utterly true, which is substantially due to the extensive investigation of a variety of sources by Jon Wyatt, is that Frederic Slater was an extremely intelligent, compassionate and highly connected person whose profession was based around a passion for finding and accurately reporting the truth.

The Real and Unreal Frederic Slater

According to the critics, Slater fails the credibility test four times over. They claim he is not an academic or scholar and does not have the observational or literacy skills to be taken seriously. He fabricated his results, he had no base or source upon which to make many sensational bogus claims. Because of these many character flaws he was neither "widely recognised"[9] nor taken seriously by his colleagues. Their problem is they have not quoted from any pre-World War 2 publication written by Slater or anyone else who is complaining about his work. Asking family members over seventy years after he passed on just doesn't measure up. What only adds to the intrigue is that even before Jon found so much more written about Slater, we already had plenty.

The information Jon found primarily related to what his family dismissively referred to as "many other areas,"[10] and in every instance he only got ticks and gold stars.

When assessing his academic prowess, it spreads all over the east coast of Australia for forty years. The first known publication written by Slater is mentioned in 1897, we are not sure of the content but assume when referencing the title, *Sea Foam and Passion Flowers*, it was either fictional or poetic. In the first decade of the twentieth century, he had two poems published in Rockhampton Capricorn along with composing two comedic operas (Nell of the Navy and Whirl of the World in 1908), but these are merely entrees for the main literary event. In another press clipping Jon sent us there is the mention of "another book entitled "The Sins of the Fathers." The book will be in the hands of Messrs Angus and Robinson next."[11] His skills in writing were considerable and diverse and from just before the turn of the twentieth century till halfway through the 1930's, Slater was the editor and chief journalist of four newspapers. Beginning in 1898 at Charters Towers, then Gulgong, followed by a longer stint at Gladstone, then another step up at Newcastle where he was publicly commended for doubling the paper's readership, Slater's career in being both an editor and journalist was in a constant ascent. So much so that after his success at Newcastle he was offered and accepted a post as a senior journalist in the Sydney Sun. In what was another surprise Slater also wrote for the opposing Sydney tabloid. This was yet another successful posting, as he was referred to in the press as a "well-known Sydney journalist,"[12] and more importantly from our perspective, the public knew him as not just a journalist but also "the man who could interpret Aboriginal picturegraphs."[13]

It is nigh on impossible to understand how it is that today it is agreed amongst his many critics, Slater was an uneducated nobody desperately trying to attract attention by any means available. But the truth is he is four times an editor and six times a journalist of the highest calibre. We have more than thirty individual clippings mentioning his name, and not once is their doubt, critique or vilification to be found. It has to be remembered that the pre-World War 2 press in Australia was more focussed on passing on what really happened and less prone to blur fact, drama and opinion. He can only have reached this level of literacy skill and public recognition if he was educated, which means by association he was an academic and scholar, and well-known at that!

Then again, some journalists frequent seedy locations and deal with shady characters, so of itself his vocation and leisure time certainly confirms his academic authenticity, but what of his moral fibre? We are assured by the academics of today that this man did distort and manipulate. If so, we should next determine the calibre of Slater's personal life, and one way of doing that is to find out who are his closest associates and friends. There is on old somewhat crude saying that states you cannot hang around dogs without getting fleas. The same applies here, if Slaters closest contacts have issues of propriety and integrity under question, then it is reasonable to assume the same applies to Slater.

An Archbishop, Headmaster, Architect, Chartered Accountant, Solicitor and .....

Slater had many colleagues who all held positions at the highest level. That makes sense, as being a writer of poems and operatic comedy is not the province of the lower class, but exclusively entertained by those of standing and education. It is not so much the impressive rollcall of those mentioned publicly as his associates that is so striking, but more the controlling role he held in every press report, as they are doing his bidding. These people are giving their free time to spend countless hours collecting data and observations out in the bush while examining Original archaeology, and in particular the picturegrams, then sending it off to Slater for him to solely determine what it meant. They have no say in the content, Slater is 'running the show' from the comfort of his armchair and all these people regard him as the final arbitrator. There is no renumeration, it is all volunteer.

After the extremely positive reception he received from a gathering of scientists attending the 1937 Australian and New Zealand Science Congress when reading the academic paper,[14] he and his close friend Roy Goddard co-wrote, he went out of his way to thank those who spent so much time compiling and copying picturegrams and symbols while trekking through some very sharp and thorny bushes. As discussed in the previous chapter in a published newspaper article written by Slater he praised Mr. W. J. Enright who was a solicitor and the President of the Anthropological Society of Sydney, Roy H. Goddard a chartered accountant and Carlyle Greenwell, an architect.[15] These people are the 'cream' of the Sydney professional elite and were highly regarded.

All his interpretations and comparisons made at the Standing Stones site somewhere near Mullumbimby, solely came about due to months of extensive on-site observations and diagrams compiled by Fred Fordham. Fordham was the headmaster of Brunswick Heads Primary School, and once again his status in this country town would have been equal to that of a doctor or judge. As with the others, Fordham is an academic and certainly not prone to associate with people of dubious character. He sacrificed over a year of his free time at the site and reported back to Slater over eighteen months. We know this is true, as we have eighteen dated letters Slater wrote back in answering Fordham's questions and often provided the meanings of symbols, lines and stone arrangements referenced from Eliza Dunlop's Original First Language interpretative 'how-to' manual.

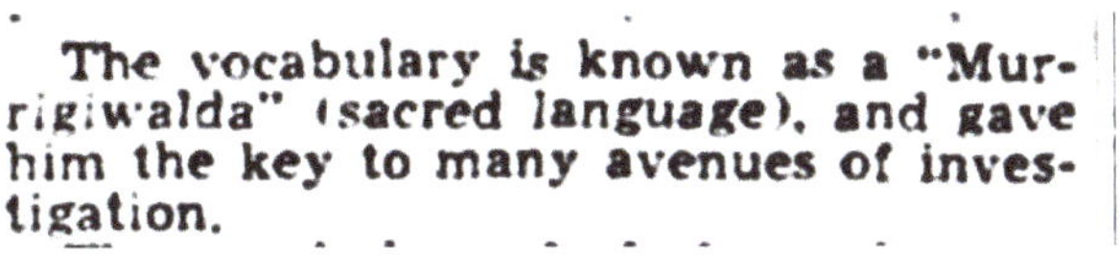

> The vocabulary is known as a "Murrigiwalda" (sacred language), and gave him the key to many avenues of investigation.

Figure 13: Murree Gwalda the How-To Manual[16]

Why would all these highly educated academics waste their time, trust and respect on a liar and cheat? This is a pivotal contradiction if accepting the current denial of Slater's virtue and academic skills, why would all these intelligent men be so naïve and blind to his devious intentions? Unless, all these men who are clearly well-off, acquired their wealth through deception and criminal activity. What if this came about through illegal or immoral activities kept secret, perhaps they were all in on this ruse. For whatever reason be it ever so infinitesimally remote, they may have conspired as a team in this charade. But for this to be true, there is still one more close associate and friend to Frederic Worral Slater that must be included in consideration before passing judgment.

The Black Bishop Tries to Capture the White King

In a fascinating and surely unexpected move in 1906 the Catholic Archbishop Moran[17] who was based in Sydney released an extremely contentious document with an accompanying commentary he endorsed, but was certainly no less than co-written with Frederic Slater. It was called the "Discovery of Australia by De Quito in the year of 1606," and central to its claims was that a Spanish Flag was raised at Port Curtis (present-day Gladstone) in 1606 and the entire continent was formally proclaimed to be the possession of principally the Holy Catholic Church and also included the current European Catholic patron Philip III of Spain[18]. The full declaration of this continent being a Catholic protectorate of Spain was printed in the document, along with a very compelling historical and archaeological case which we have no doubt was assembled and written by Slater.

Figure 14: King Philip III[19]

Their association begins in 1899 at Gladstone when the Archbishop of Sydney met Slater who "presented him with a commemorative edition of the Gladstone Advocate."[20] All of this was also extensively covered in the Catholic Voice. As to why Cardinal Moran met with Slater is never stated or hinted at the time, but within a decade it becomes crystal clear that Slater had no choice but to take "off the mask and carry the baton."[21] What needs to be appreciated is that Moran wasn't just another Catholic priest, he was the first Cardinal stationed in Australia. Such was his standing and importance that when he died it is estimated that over 250,000 people paid their respects at his funeral. That is close to half the population of Sydney and clearly not all were Catholics. That Moran was a close friend and associate of Slater speaks volumes about Slater's integrity, character and respect.

Figure 15: Patrick Cardinal Moran, Archbishop of Sydney[22]

Until Cardinal Moran died in 1911, he kept championing the notion that it was not a British Protestant Cook, but a Spanish Catholic by the name of De Quito[23] who discovered and legally claimed this country to be a Spanish colony. There already existed a religious division of considerable degree within Australia, and the archbishop was certainly adding 'fuel to the fire.' Knowing he was getting on in years, we have little doubt he was tolerated in his personal crusade until his inevitable demise, and that should be the end of such inconveniences.

Figure 16: Pedro Fernández de Quirós[24]

What they did not factor into their expectations was Slater's contributions. In 1912, using the paper he edited as his media outlet, he started publishing his archaeological investigations in the Port Curtis area. He found the remains of "three Spanish cannons"[25] and "a small galleon wreck."[26] What was also mentioned was the comparisons he made between Port Curtis and main inlet at the New Hebrides, which was part of the paper the archbishop released in 1906. The reason he made this comparison was simply because De Quito was the principal captain of three Spanish ships and in his written report, he made mention of the place they dropped anchor which was larger than all of Europe and Asia Minor and could supply safe anchorage for one thousand boats. He also made note of the abundance of black obsidian rocks and a large outcrop of marble. During his fifty-four day stay De Quito named this continent The Holy Ghost of Australia and actually proclaimed himself as the first king.

And that is where the troubles and lies began. De Quito had already offended his second-in-charge Luís Vaz de Torres[27] (Torres Strait was named by him). Torres wanted two members of his crew whipped for a minor indiscretion, but De Quito had a far more compassionate nature and refused, instead transferring both to his crew. Torres was to say the least miffed, and because the ships were separated by storms during the return journey and Torres returned first, he had the ear of Philip and set about sullying De Quito and marginalising everything he did. It was Torres who denied De Quito found such a massive southern continent and it was Torres who first suggested it was not a huge land mass but the Islands of New Hebrides.

Figure 17: Luís Vaz de Torres[28]

Even though the largest harbour in the New Hebrides could barely accommodate fifty ships, that there is no obsidian or marble anywhere and it is certainly not larger than all of Europe, or even half of Malta, Philip never bothered to read De Quito's diary or journal when he finally did return to Spain. What Slater did was to read his account then find the only harbour that could, according to the first British report on Port Curtis, have the capacity to provide safe anchorage for one-thousand ships. Every feature described could be ticked off at Port Curtis and was lacking at the New Hebrides. Slater mentioned all these glaring comparative inconsistencies in the original paper released by Cardinal Moran.

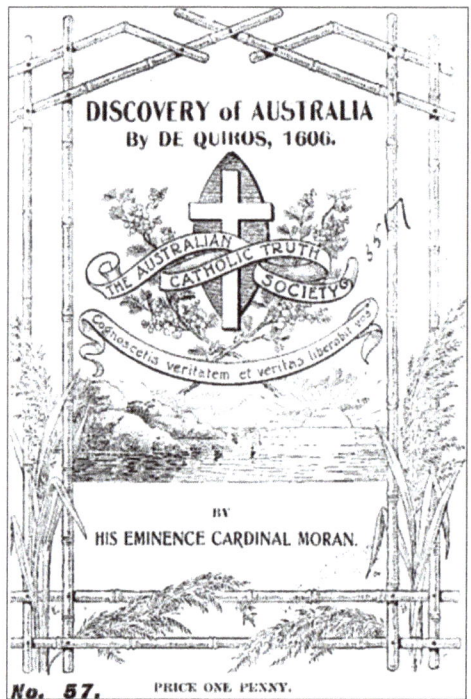

Figure 18: Cardinal Moran's Paper on De Quiros[29]
(See: Appendix for copy of this paper)

He never let up, and even though for some time little publicity was given after the Archbishop of Sydney died, Slater made sure it was still bubbling somewhere near the surface. Then in 1936 the Mitchell Library bought and catalogued De Quito's report ("Relecion de Don de Pito"). For the first time in any press clipping, we see the first printed evidence of another expert disagreeing with Slater. It needs to be pointed out this disagreement did not extend into his Original picturegram translations but was centred on one entry in De Quito's journal where he referred to dwellings near the beach that had palm-frond thatched rooves. The critic was adamant that as Original tribes did not build houses or permanent buildings this truth disqualifies any notion he raised the Spanish flag in Australia.

He is manifestly wrong, as the remains of many quite elaborate permanent stone buildings can be found at Lake Condah and James Cook spoke of sighting a permanent building with a roof measuring seventy yards in length and four yards wide which was constructed at Shelley Beach (Ballina, N.S.W.). We believe this continued championing of the notion that the Protestant British Lieutenant did not discover Australia, but it was Catholic Spanish Captain who raised the flag over one-hundred-and-fifty years earlier, did Slater no favours and the time was soon coming where he would be held accountable.

"Cancelled"[30]

In one press clipping it refers to a time when Slater was asked by archaeologists to come down to interpret a series of rock engravings at Maroota that had defied all attempts over the last twenty-years to be understood. According to the article it took Slater ten minutes to do so, and no-one at the site questioned the result or his credentials. The Manly Council paid Slater to translate some Aboriginal writings somewhere close to the main beach. Slater was invited to speak at the Royal Anthropological Society in 1934 and the Sydney Anthropological Society in 1935. He co-wrote the Burragurra paper in 1937 which was well received at the Science Congress in 1937, as mentioned previously twenty-two months later the same paper was censored by Sydney University and stamped cancelled.

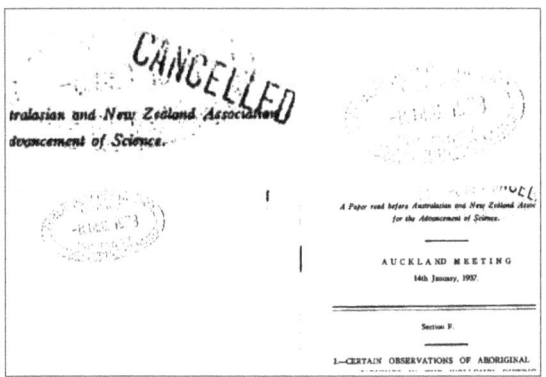

Figure 19: Cover Page of Goddard & Slater's Paper[31]

What is fascinating is that the paper has not one but three stamps, the front page detailing the contents has the cancelled stamp and the Sydney University faculty responsible, "Tropical Medicine and Public Health."[32] But when turning the page to the first section written by Goddard that describes the site, geology and setting but does not mention the interpretations, it is given a stamp of approval. However, further on where Slater begins his passage describing what this means a second cancelled stamp covers the heading. One could question as to what expertise a medical faculty has in archaeology, and the answer is at best minimal.

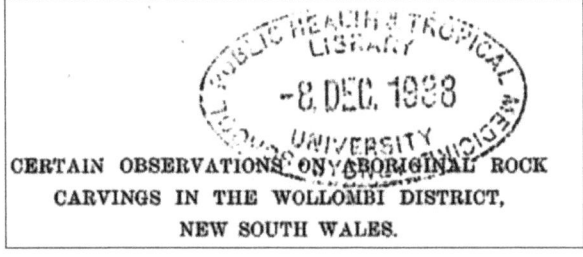

Figure 20: Tropical Medicine and Public Health Cancelled Stamp[33]

In his personal Standing Stones correspondence to Fordham during 1939 he advises Fordham not to trust anyone from the Government, Australian Museum, or in particular, Sydney University. What is clear is that the Australian coast is no longer clear, and the mud is beginning to fly towards one target.

The Sins of Omission, Addition and Contrition

Until Jon had sent his research to us, we had originally assumed that Slater's talk of off-world beings coming to Earth and specifying that some were actually born elsewhere in the Cosmos was the main reason he was attacked and marginalised. However, with so much printed evidence at our disposal it is now one of at least six 'transgressions' Slater was responsible for, and in all probability, it would be ranked sixth.

'First cab off the rank' is most likely to be Slater's decision to carry Cardinal Moran's Catholic baton. In insisting Cook did not discover Australia, this raises legal issues that have a distinctly Spanish setting. Not far behind is Slater's insistence that the Original people, who were tallied in the 1965 National Census as non-human fauna, were part of an ancient civilisation that was the pinnacle of human existence. He then adds more in including that these people were the first on the planet and were the source for all global religions, the base for all languages, philosophies, numeration and so he continued. In adding to the cultural discomfort, he claimed he was able to read the meaning behind all Stone Age engravings and paintings as he had access to the 'key' that can unlock their hidden meanings. Slater then turned his attention to huge amount of Egyptian-linked archaeology in Australia, insisting that their culture, religion and hieroglyphs was also sourced from Australia.

Then past all of these uncomfortable comparisons mention is made of Aliens coming from distant constellations and then advising and guiding humans in Australia. Our take is that if this topic was not mentioned it would have made no difference, the other five indiscretions were more than enough to see him being slandered and vilified. At best, this Alien inclusion is merely 'icing on the cake.'

There is ample evidence that Slater was undeniably a radical academic, regardless, his work satisfies the highest scholarly standards required and his sources were the best available. With the questions over his skill, intentions and character fully dispensed with, all that is left is to read his work first then make a decision as to whether he is correct. The problem is if he is telling the truth, then virtually everything we thought we knew about humanities past and purpose is not the truth.

In that pursuit, we will now present his opening introduction: an overview of some of the main avenues of his interpretations of the real history of ancient Australia.

Chapter 4

"THE PHARAOHS OF THE SOUTH LAND" BY FREDERIC SLATER

"Stone Age man has presented problems to the anthropologist and the archaeologist which have led them into side tracks which, unlike the open highway that goes on and on, have ended in a veil of mystery. Evolutionary theories as fantastic as mythologies of ancient nations, have proved no better than the adoption as gods of such mystic personification as Osiris, Horus, Baal, Zeus, Jupiter or Thor, under which nomenclatures men of profound knowledge concealed the truth of man's being. The symbolisation of the elements, in the age when methods of recording were in the making, led to the deification of imaginary and real people. There the simple beginning of mankind has been involved in fantasy almost inextricable. Gradually those that have kept the highway have deciphered the direction posts which man from the beginning of time left for future generations. The era of history in which we are living dates from our ability to read these directions. Gradually we are expanding the period. From 4,004 B.C. we have got back to 40,000 B.C. discovering in this march into the past civilizations of undoubted authenticity the records of which point the way backward still further.

Well might we ask; What is civilization? If we accept the philosophic ruling that it is the condition of advancement of nations in the material and moral development of mankind, and that there are two movements always going on in all communities: one progressive and the other retrogressive, we come up against a factor – which will be found later on in the "Book of Translations" – which may create controversy; but cannot be controverted. Man in the beginning of time had a higher sense of his duty to man and the development of life – which to him was the soul – than can be found in the cultured nations of 2,000 years ago or the nations of today. There never was a time since mankind came into the world that civilisation had not a place in his philosophy of life. Stone Age Man, who saw the beginning of life, did not just lie down and die leaving his bones for anthropologists to make learned discourse about and dress up in flesh according to their ideas of the evolution of man; or the implements of stone called rude and crude and savage, but which were all that were necessary for their simple needs. Primordial man could write. He recorded the history of time and the history of the world from man's advent when the earth was prepared for him.

The records of the Stone Age Australians the remnants of which still survive, are the same as those of other Stone Age Men, records that have been the despair of anthropologists and archaeologists. All know that they are records; but the method of deciphering they failed to discover. They are lost in a multiplicity of languages and the culture of races that have come after them. The key will be found in these pages. The Scribes of the Stone Age carry the world's history back 150,000 years at least. They establish the connecting link between the ancient people of the Nilotic region and the earliest life of man in a world that had a revealed knowledge of how it was created and how man came into being.

"The Pharaohs of the South Land" is not a poetic nimbus set round the head of kings of most ancient renown. It is used in a more primordial sense. It denotes the royal estates when the world was a great house and mankind emerged from the gateway of the Nilotic region in the dawn of time. To the southern part of the domain came a grand pageant on the rocks, as though on the leaves of a book, primordial man wrote the story of the Creation and Destiny of Man.

Archaeologists who have for centuries followed the beaten track in the Northern Hemisphere, verifying the records of ancient historians, have little idea of the wealth of records awaiting the investigator in Australia. The youngest of the continents it was left with a geological formation that confronted when he commenced his exodus from the creative centre of his primordial being with a flora and fauna that is only found in fossils in formations below the surface in other countries. Here are preserved the remnants of primitive mankind whose ancestors had made countless centuries of history when the Babylonians were baking bricks on which were recorded the history of their own times; when Odin, Thor and Loki were gathering the heroes into Valhalla, and Egypt was evolving its mythology and eschatology from the animistic philosophy of those ancient men, picking out from the so called rude and crude pictures on the rocks the ideographs to form the hieroglyphics.

Chaldea, Phoenicia, Greece, Rome: nations that were world sojourners and conquerors. What were they compared with these wanderers of the Palaeolithic and Neolithic ages of the Nilotic origin? They set forth to gather food along unbeaten tracks and have remained food gatherers to this day. They were ancient settlers in Australia when Herodotus referred to the cave dwellers as the only people who could cross the Sahara Desert alone. The natives of Australia are descendants of the same primitive people. Dwellers in caves and food gatherers they still travel over desert country for days without water with nothing to guide them but the knowledge which they had acquired from the world's first invention known as Boonigeroo – the guide to truth – and the origin of the compass. This will be explained in the Book of Translations and the Book of Searchings.

Wanderers of this self-same stock have been the parents of nations spread far and wide whose people have evolved religions and philosophies, spread culture and written history, developed science and invention. In Australia they have remained food gatherers with no higher ambition than to be left alone to live the life their fathers lived, to follow the teachings of the philosophy of Animism – belief in the Hidden Creator of whom the world knew 250,000 years ago, and the belief in the soul, in the spirit immortal and imperishable.

Their simple faith – they knew the Light of Heaven as the Soul of the Earth – was the formation of the Egyptian Book of the Dead, the philosophy of Kon-fu-tse of China, the religion of the Akkadians who evolved cuneiform writing by means of which has been recorded rich records of science, history, poetry and religion. They sort not after false gods, nor did they know of them, but they left the records of their own lives sculptured on the rocks.

From the time of the earliest settlement of Europeans in Australia, the pictorial painting and sculptural art of the natives have attracted attention but even in the early days 150 years ago, nothing could be learned concerning them. A mysterious veil has covered them. Anthropologists made notes but went no further than to say that they had a meaning. That meaning was lost in antiquity, as in the case of similar drawings in other parts of the world.

In the march of civilisations these antiquities have not completely been swept away even in the centres of population. The environments of Sydney, New South Wales, with its population verging on 1,500,000 still have some of them preserved. From the lofty tower of the General Post Office – the carving on which have been immortalised by Ruskin in his best vein of sarcasm more bitting than which he applied to the celebrated work of Whistler, can be seen places hidden by a fringe of bush – still the forest primeval – where rock carvings by Aboriginals defy the wheels of time in more senses than one, for the wheels of vehicles, ancient and modern, have desecrated their antique loveliness. Beautified by age and the stories they tell. They are observed by passers by with comments of curiosity or derision.

We are opening the picture book. Just as Young and Champillon discovered the picture alphabet in the hieroglyphics of Egypt, these sculptures on the rock are in reality the picture language of an ancient people.

About 100 miles from Sydney on the oldest road to the north where the Main Dividing Range separates the waters of the Macdonald River that flows into the Hawkesbury River (described by Anthony Trellope as the Rhine of Australia, but called the Aboriginals Decrubun) from the waters of the Wollombi that flows into the Hunter River, there is a rare treasure house for scientists. The immense coal producing area has provided geologists of the ice age, when the earth commenced to shed its frozen garments and Pleistocian man started his trek in pursuit of animals making for colder zones. Among these signs of glacial activity are evidences of fire and the intrusion of mountains capped with basalt, once molten lava. Greater still are the evidences of swirling waters and sedimentary deposits. The ridges and flat-topped are of Hawkesbury sandstone which gives a reaction for gold of more than a grain to the ton. Here in the valley and on the mountain side the flora of the carboniferous age still flourishes and marsupials still abound. The district was a paradise for the food gathering Aborigines before the white men brought the cattle (nulka-nulka: animals with points on their foreheads. Sometimes Kumbakuluku: animals that make an angry sound) and horses (Yarraman: moving fast) among them, depriving of grass the animals they hunted and causing them to seek other pastures. The trees were also cut down and the bees had no food and left no hives to be robbed.

The caves and the rock ledges show evidence of occupation by people who left their story behind them in pictures and carvings. Many of these have been reproduced in books and have been drawn and displayed before learned societies, discussed, no more – and then left to the student the riddle of the universe and the mystery of man to elucidate. They are word-pictures sometimes of family life, records of ownership, incidence of the time, totem signs, boundary marks, showing the limits of a living area under the patriarchal system [sic] which they followed in these caves and under the rock ledges are many impressions of hands – the world wide symbol of the sun and life made by primitive man, the three fingers between the thumb and the small finger forming the hieroglyphic for the Sun of Light or Light of the World. Among the Australian Aboriginals Mu was life, and life was the soul. So the occupants of these caves left their handwriting or their sign. They had lived there as shown by the symbol of the Sun and the Son of Light. The hand was called marra and was therefore associated with life and essential with the maintenance of life.

It was not until the Great Record Book was discovered and the whole incident of the ritual revealed in their own language and translated into English, that the full importance of these pictures on the rocks was revealed."[1]

Chapter 5

CIVILISED BEHAVIOUR

Slater's opening chapter, along with three that follow, is more about setting the scene in summarising a change in global perspectives, order and priorities. The reason why he spends so much time setting out a framework before presenting the supporting evidence is simply due to the enormity of the task he is undertaking. He is basically stating that literally everything written and postulated in relation to human evolution and pre-history is wrong. It is a huge call, and as much of what he insists is fact is challenging verging on ridiculous for many, it must be remembered that while we only have the draft complete replete with crossed out lines with hundreds of additions written in ink, the final copy was approved to be published by a reputable publishing house in London. From an Australian Pre-World War 2 academic viewpoint, to be accepted for publication in London is the 'holy grail.' The editors involved would be no less cognisant of the sensational claims Slater based his book upon and must have been convinced that the body of work and academic rigour applied was convincing and logical.

"The Pharaohs of the South Land"[1]

In Slater's introduction he focuses on two fundamental and revolutionary concepts and the ongoing impact this has had on humanity. He begins by redefining what most would assume to be an unambiguous term that chronicles how modern humans have so badly misunderstood our purpose for existing. There is a common belief that when using the word civilisation, it refers to technological progress, larger cities and perhaps a more compassionate and genteel form of personal behaviour. Whereas the opposite term of primitive is technologically cruder, less refined and certainly lacking in intelligence or grace. Slater sees what most assume to be factual in reverse. When posing the question, "what is civilisation,"[2] he nominates two opposing elements that relate to "the material and moral development of mankind."[3] He is adamant "that there are two movements always going on in all communities: one progressive and the other retrogressive."[4] Slater openly concedes this interplay "may create controversy; but cannot be controverted."[5]

From Slater's viewpoint civilisation is devoted to the betterment of the soul, everything else is secondary. He believed that "man in the beginning of time had a higher sense of his duty to man and the development of life-which to him was the soul-than can even be found in the cultured nations of 2,000 years ago or the nations of today."[6]

Not only does Slater believe that ancient primitive societies were more evolved, the records they left behind in their art and engravings was actually all part of a global language of which he has the skills and references to enable a totally exact translation to be made.

Slater is adamant that the Old Ones knew all about our evolution, ancient history and reasons why we exist. His research is unequivocal, in that Australia was the base upon which philosophy, religion, culture, art and the nobler aspects of humanity originated.

The recurring problem was that at the same time Slater was saying and writing such sensational statements. Original people in Australia had no personal or legal rights, were not recognised in the national census as being human, could not vote in elections and most were locked up in missions, reserves or jails. Many academics declared them to be the most primitive peoples of the planet and had assumed they were in the process of being genetically overwhelmed until becoming extinct. In concocting a false legal doctrine of Terra Nullius, that denial of worth or authenticity of all Australian Original societies means that these people supposedly lived in a way so primitive and unstructured that it was literally an embarrassment for all who believe that 'clothes maketh the man'.

The Issue of Timing and Placement

In this introductory chapter there is an issue of numbers and places. Slater opens with the traditional biblical date of 4004 BC, which he clearly dismisses then pushes the dates back to 40,000 BC. However, further on he mentions dates of 150,000 years and then goes back even further to 250,000 years. Dates like these are still a huge call and more accurate than any other timing suggested by his contemporaries. On both occasions these ancient dates relate to the Original people being part of the very first race which Slater identifies as being Egyptian. We must bear in mind that Slater is relying on the science available in the 1930's, which is lacking in Carbon 14[7], OSL[8], Thermoluminescence[9] and mtDNA[10].

Equally, his insistence that Original people are linked to their Egyptian ancestors, is clouded by one glaring omission, Atlantis. Egypt is a very recent rebound from Atlantis, and the reason Slater is so aligned to Egypt is simply because talk of Atlantis was literally non-existent when he was looking for the ultimate truths. Of course, it is known today that any six-figured date is clearly outside any Egyptian involvement, but when it comes to Atlantis the timing is perfect.

Figure 21: Atlantis[11]

Slater also makes mention of Australia being the "youngest of the continents,"[12] which is actually the reverse, but once again all of these errors in timing and location are totally excusable then and 'par for any course' if living in the 1930's.

Having dispensed with these incidental errors, with everything else Slater reports and interprets there is no need to equivocate or moderate. He is on song and totally correct in content, wisdom revealed and historical authenticity.

"The Great Record Book"[13]

The real crux of Slater's research, that he had an unfettered access to Eliza Dunlop's book detailing the First Original and Global Language (Murree Gwalda) is not in question. Slater concludes his opening chapter in boldly declaring that "it was not until the Great Record Book was discovered and the whole incident of the ritual revealed in their own language and translated into English that the full importance of these pictures on the rocks was revealed."[14]

Yes, Roy Goddard was Dunlop's great grandson and knew what she wrote was just too sensational for him or anyone else, but Slater, the question still remains as to what was it about Slater that made him the only candidate worthy of being given the Great Record Book?

At no stage does Slater directly address why he alone could accept this ancient 'baton,' but there is one observation he made that makes it crystal clear this was a task that Slater alone deserved. When referring to picturegrams still visible near Sydney, which he compared "to the celebrated work of Whistler,"[15] Slater was entranced by the depth, insights and sublime wisdom engraved into the rocks, "where rock carvings by the Aboriginals defy the wheels of time in more senses than one, for the wheels of vehicles, ancient and modern, have desecrated their antique loveliness. Beautified by age and the stories they tell. They are observed by passers by with comments of curiosity and derision."[16] This man can feel the past, he can sense the depth of these profound teachings that resonates throughout every site, and the Spirits know he alone is "opening the picture book,"[17] simply because they knew he was the only white-fella on the planet who was deserving of unravelling this enormous treasure-trove of everything.

The Content of the Grand Pageant

The title of Slater's first chapter, "The Pharaohs of the South Land"[18] is deliberately enigmatic as it "is not a poetic nimbus set round head of kings of most ancient renown."[19] It is meant to be symbolic "in a more primordial sense."[20] From Slater's interpretation "it denotes the royal estates when the world was a great house … in the dawn of time."[21] Slater is adamant that in these first times nothing was hidden, especially so in Australia. For it was here "came a grand pageant. On the rocks, as though on the leaves of a book, primordial man wrote the story of Creation and the Destiny of Man."[22]

What Slater is claiming is that this venerable knowledge of human purpose and destiny is not only real but never left the planet. And all of the keys will be found within the book Slater had written. From an historical, philosophical and spiritual stance no-one has ever made such a monumental claim. As sensational as this may seem, it is underpinned by one radical foundation point that no academic, until Slater, had made. His research has convinced him that "the records of the Stone Age Australians, the remnants of which still survive, are the same as those of other Stone Age Men."[23]

Whether comparing Rome, Greece, Confucius, the Egyptian Book of the Dead[24] or some other cultural icon, whatever is offered invariably pales by comparison to the Australian counterpart. If civilisation is all about developing the soul, then way back at the start in Australia was as good as it ever was. He has no doubt after consulting the Great Record Book that "man in the beginning of time had a higher sense of his duty to man and the development of life."[25]

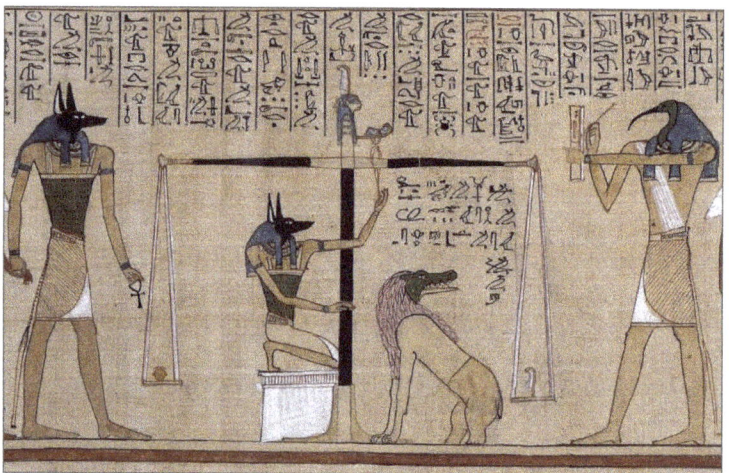

Figure 22: Egyptian Book of the Dead[26]

Babylon, Troy or a Rough Leaking Stick and Bark Lean-to in the Bush.

If I was to set a question in a history exam and ask the student to select from these three choices as to which answer best illustrates what the word civilisation means, nearly every, if not every, student would choose Babylon or Troy. Slater would fail the exam in choosing the Original shack and lose the right to call himself a scholar, which is exactly what happens today.

But this would not be the only question Slater would fail in selecting the approved answer. Today all students must say that humans evolved on this planet. Slater not only claims that humans "came to Earth ... with his senses (seven of them),"[27] but went further in not only insisting that "primordial man could write. He recorded the history of time and the history of the world from man's advent when the Earth was prepared for him."[28] Advent means "coming into place"[29] and "arrival,"[30] if somewhere is preparing for your arrival that automatically means you came from somewhere other than this planet, Earth. That is yet another red cross in Slater's exam paper of supposed historical facts, and there are plenty more crosses ahead.

The problem Slater faced then, and still does now, is that those experts who set the content for all exams have never seen or read the Great Record Book or any of Slater's written work, deny he was a scholar and refuse to do one skerrick of research into his past. They set an exam on topics of which they know nothing, have no questions to ask and no inclination but to do anything beyond more of the same. While these critics know nothing of "a world that had a revealed knowledge of how it was created and how man came into being,"[31] it is so fortunate Slater knows all about such vital concerns and all that is required is to read all about it.

Chapter 6

"WORDS ON THE ROCKS" BY FREDERIC SLATER

"Primitive Men of the Stone Age have recorded the history of the world since the dawn of life. In parts of Australia their records can be found in sculpture on the rocks and in caves and under ledges of rock where they dwelt. They were guided in their work by the material they possessed; but only where they carved on the rock did they give an imperishable record and guidelines to the generations that came after them. In few centres of this primitive culture can be found a more wonderful ("katabul" is the Aboriginal word) library and gallery of art as in the Wollombi district. From time to time scraps of records from this area – almost as primeval as when the white man found it, have appeared in the books written by anthropologists or shown at Scientific Societies' meetings. But none have revealed the colossal work on the Mountain Top at Burragurra, which means "Writing on the Rock" or "Rock with Words". It was so called on the maps by the early surveyors who opened up the first great road to the north of Australia. Burragurra stands out prominently on a spur of the main Dividing Range separating the waters flowing into the Hawkesbury, from those flowing into the Hunter, the former to the South, the later to the North. Possibly the sight was chosen ideographically as illustrating part of the sacred rites and symbols which were left to their care, to be expressed in a syllabic language, and by means of signs and pictorial symbols. Locally the Mountain Top is known as "Devil's Rock". This was probably the inference drawn by the early settlers from the description of the place given to them by Aborigines who feared an intrusion on their sacred preserves. "Word" and "Evil" (in Aboriginal language) being somewhat similar in sound. But the word for what we call "Devil" and which the Aborigines learned to call "Debbil Debbil" was "Dinna-yaree" a beast (or evil one) held down by the foot.

Whatever may have been the cause of it Burragurra has remained in comparative isolation for more than 100 years. The sculpture is worn and battered by storms – for it is up in the snow clouds in winter, and is swept by bush fires in the torrid heat of summer. Yet it has kept its record in writing. The Book of Knowledge 150,000 years old is now being opened up for all to read.

During the months of August, 1935 Mr. Walter Enright, a lawyer of Maitland who has discovered innumerable pieces of rock sculpture and picture graphs in the Wollombi, and has been associated with many scientists in exploring these regions; and Mr. R. H. Goddard chartered accountant and an authority on Australian Aboriginal artifacts, under took an expedition to Burragurra.

The log of the expedition written and drawn by Mr. Goddard gives in accurate detail the wonders of scenery and records of antiquity. …

(See: Chapter 14 & Appendix 2 - A complete account of Goddard's report is given at the end of this book. It has not been included now as the writing is drier and more scientific and completely different from that of Slater's work.)

I have not interfered with Mr. Goddard's description of the figures found on the rock for he uses the same descriptive language concerning them as anthropologists of importance and eminence have used.

What is the meaning of it all? Emu pads, grotesque figures, strange animals, circles, wavey lines, strokes and innumerable other indefinite things. Just words! Syllables that were the beginning of words when language was in the making. It is a great story of the beginning of time in an immense book covering acres of ground."[1]

Chapter 7

WOLLOMBI AND GOSFORD: HOME BASE

Possibly the reason Slater maintains that this area is 'ground-central' is because the Great Record Book was compiled by Eliza Dunlop in consultation with a Wollombi Elder, or it could be because this area has the most numerous and intensive collection of rock-art/picturegrams in the world, for whatever the reason the second chapter is all about one very important site near the Wollombi called Burragurra.

      Slater not only reminds the reader of the gravitas on what can be interpreted which includes "the history of the world since the dawn of life,"[1] but adds a level of foresight and intent that is quite radical. He is adamant that they created "an imperishable record and guidance to the generations that came after them."[2] Slater believed our ancient ancestors knew their wisdom was deep and essential to future generations, and that it would always be under threat. And in that pursuit "few centres of this primitive culture can be found a more wonderful … library and gallery of art as in the Wollombi district."[3] Of all the many sites and engravings of this area Slater believed that there is one site that was first amongst equals, which features "the colossal work on the Mountain Top at Burragurra, which means 'Writing on the Rock' or 'Rock with Words.'"[4]

Figure 23: Burragurra[5]

Eighty Years Later

For quite some time all our work in the Gosford-Wollombi region had no connection to anything Slater wrote or observed, granted we did have Slater's personal notes and instructions relating to the Standing Stones site, and occasional refences were made to archaeology in the Gosford region, but until receiving a copy of the archaeological paper he and Goddard wrote on Burragurra we did not know of any substantial connection. More to the point, we had virtually completed over 90% of all the work done in the Gosford region before first stumbling on to Slater's work at the Standing Stones site.

To begin with the only thing we shared with Slater were the same two conclusions, we got there through completely different paths and localities, but irrespective of how we arrived at the same destination it seemed very clear so much of the archaeology in the area had an Egyptian and/or Off-world Alien imprint. The very first mention of ancient Egyptians in this area was never ours but that of the Senior Park Ranger of Brisbane Waters, John Gallard, (who has recently passed on) when he took us to a variety of sites spread in and around Gosford and the Wollombi localities.

Waiting for the Sun to Shine

This Egyptian journey all began on a very cloudy day sitting beside a site Gallard insisted was an engraving of an ankh. For some time neither Evan nor I were convinced, of the many rock engravings at this site it certainly was the most worn and indistinct, and being so cloudy only added to the indecisive state of affairs. It took close to an hour until the sun broke through, and once a trickle of water was added to the engraved lines, what was lost in the shadows returned to its former glory. John was right, not only was the shape and outline clear to see, but so too the footprint of an ibis sitting beside. The ankh[6] is an ancient Egyptian talisman held exclusively by Thoth[7], the God of Wisdom, which was confirmed by the associated fact that Thoth had two animal totems, of which one was of an ibis.

Figure 24: Ankh Engraving with Ibis footprint[8]

With the sun shining and water flowing, John then took us to view two other engravings on the same platform that shared similar Egyptian motifs. The figure of Daramulum[9], the first son of Baiame[10], was so unexpected, twice over. He was wearing what looked so much like the typical Pharaonic headdress and so unlike any Original counterpart, and what only accentuated that Egyptian modality was that his head was in profile. Normally Original human engravings have two eyes facing the viewer, until now I have never seen anything other than a full-face visage.

But if there were any doubts, once John told me the Dreaming story that accompanied this engraving, they vanished in the clear comparisons to the Egyptian myth of Isis and Osiris. In this Australian foundation myth, Daramulum was defeated by the underworld spirits and was taken, killed and cut apart, but his consort, Ngalbal[11] used her sacred shield with the magic it contained to resurrect and reconstruct her fallen male companion. This is exactly what Isis did when Osiris was vanquished in ancient Egypt.

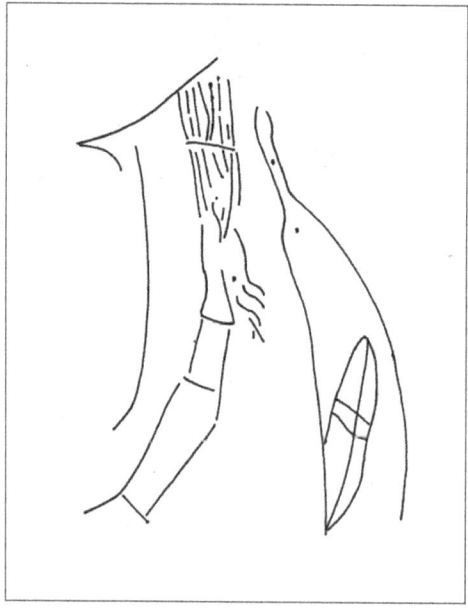

Figure 25: Daramulum's head and Ngalbal represented in emu form with her shield[12]

What is equally revealing is that this depiction has a baboon/monkey face, and Thoth's second totem form is that of a monkey. Even if this narrative is totally coincidental, which seems a very far-fetched notion with the ankh so close by, the third figure John took us to view next, leaves no room to manoeuvre anywhere but Egypt. It is a human figure adopting a pose never depicted anywhere else, except in ancient Egypt. This extremely geometric and symmetrical bodily arrangement is exactly how the Egyptian God of Inheritance must be portrayed.

Figure 26: God of Inheritance (Rock Engraving & Glyph Comparison)[13]

Another Profiled Ibis/Human

If we needed more proof (which we didn't) John made sure we left with clarity and no room for doubt. The next site we visited is not far away in distance but so similar in inspiration and presentation. Again, in a unique profiled stance, this human with an ibis head has a club foot which is an obligatory disability that the son of Baiame, Daramulum must be depicted.

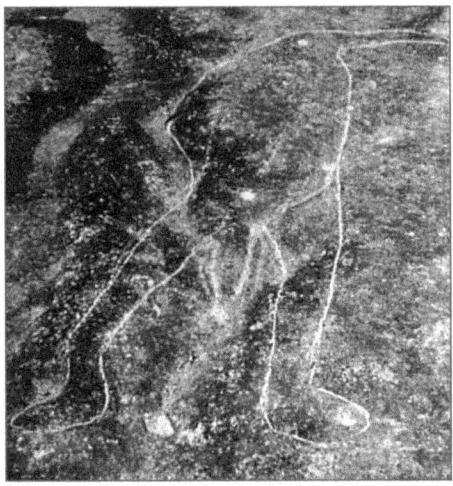

Figure 27: Rock Engraving Daramulum[14]

It was only after this four-part introduction into archaeology with a distinctly ancient Egyptian flavour was completed, did John Gallard raise the possibility of visiting the somewhat notorious and controversial Kariong hieroglyphs. We knew of the disputes and acrimonious climate of the site, and to be honest saw them as 'damaged goods' and most likely irretrievable, but after some prompting from John we did provisionally agree to attend and view.

Figure 28: Hieroglyphs at Bambara/Kariong[15]

We now fully believe that the carvings are legitimate, but to begin with they were of a secondary concern, it was more the peripheral archaeology that attracted our attention and helped validate the hieroglyphs. Just behind the three walls with over 300 hieroglyphs is an artificial tunnel of ten metres in length. For some time NPWS experts falsely claimed it was a natural formation, but knowing that to be an utterly ridiculous position to maintain, recently conceded that it is indeed a human-made construction and have determined it was the outcome of the efforts of unknown and unnamed 'vandals.' They not only extracted tonnes and tonnes of sandstone, but then removed the tailings, excavated rocks and crumbling sandstone, and during the entire process no-one saw or heard anything.

Figure 29: The Shaft[16]

This is remotely possible, but without a name, photograph of any stage in excavation or stat dec admitting culpability or a reason for doing this, the chances this is all a hoax are minimal. The problem is Aunty Minnie Mace picked up two objects right next to the entrance of the tunnel and both were heavily coated in soil and looked like two clumps of dirt. Aunty Minnie was called by the Guardian Spirits to pick up these objects, and it was only after they were taken home and the dirt was removed was the truth clear to see.

It is one thing to allege the tunnel was made recently with mischievous intent but to claim both an ancient human bone (as identified through a cat-scan) and a metal object of which 24% of the content that cannot be matched to any entry on the Earthly Periodic Table, was planted there as bogus extras is bad science and impossible. The experts from a local University Laboratory are adamant that one quarter of whatever this metal is, does not belong to this planet.

Figure 30: Bone Artefact[17]

Figure 31: Metal Artefact[18]

Crossing the Divide

The same non-Earthly location applies to the rock engravings at a site called Bulgandry. Both Aunty Beve and Elder Gavi Duncan have stood at this site and shared the Dreaming Story of travelling across "the Milky Way"[19] in a spaceship which his foot rests upon. That he holds the sun and moon in his hands, as does Thoth, is not a coincidence.

Figure 32: Bulgandry[20]

I remember asking Aunty Beve why was it that all the human-like figures engraved in the area never have any form of neck. It seems like they are wearing helmets of some sort. She was very quick in correcting the term I used immediately substituting my description of a helmet for "hats."²¹ She was adamant that was the term the Elders used and that is what they wore. She also made it clear that the belt that runs across the waist of Bulgandry was indeed the "Belt of Orion."²²

Figure 33: Diagram of Bulgandry (Belt of Orion)²³

The selection of beings wearing hats are the norm, and what needs to be appreciated is the same type of hat is worn at Burragurra. There is a being there that from the very first sighting we referred to as an Alien, and it was at least ten years later before we first read Slater's paper on Burragurra and it came as no surprise to discover the entire rock platform is about the first arrival via a space ship of Baiame and his family. What did catch us a touch unprepared was that this introductory chapter on Burragurra contains Goddard's field notes, which can also be found in the part of the paper he co-wrote, but there is nothing in this chapter relating to Slater's interpretation. It could appear further on, and as we have not read the entire book, it may still turn up, but knowing how sensational his interpretation of the site is, just leaving first mention of Goddard's report lacking in any explanation from Slater is a touch perplexing. Whether it does turn up later or was omitted due to such talk of Aliens arriving on this planet being just too far a stretch, we feel some of what he wrote in the report read out at 1937 Science Congress really does need to be mentioned in detail now.

Although quite an extensive report, there are two sections that warrant further reflection. As such, we feel opening this brief introduction with what follows after Slater stated that "I hope to make it clear by interpreting the words on the rock at Burragurra"²⁴ is necessary.

"The story goes that Bhaiame first made two men, one of them he called Boobardy (the word means father). He also placed one woman in the world, giving her the name of Numbardy. He put the men in a deep sleep, from which they awoken in the prime of life.

They found themselves surrounded by a glorious game abounding taurai. One of them refused to understand his circumstances and would not kill and eat the game. Boobardy, finding that the other man was dying, shifted his camp, taking with him his consort, Numbardy. Afterwards Boobardy went to the spot where he found the other man dying, and, to his great surprise, found that he had vanished. Upon examining the ground he discovered a footprint and then came across others. It was a print of the right foot. Boobardy, developing the instinct of the tracker, followed the footprint until he saw his comrade walking ahead and called out to him, "Turrawula ngai dhurudi' ("Come back, my friend"). But the nameless one who had left the footprints (since called Mundowa) pointed to the setting sun and said, "Yugar ngutta" ("Not I: I go that way").

"Ngutta Ngintabe your" ("I will go with you"), cried Boobardy. But the unknown figure went on until he came to a tree huge in girth and so tall that the foliage mingled with the clouds. Picking up a suitable stone he cut notches into the trunk of the tree and so climbed up, calling to Boobardy, "Turrawulla, Turrawulla, guiya ngaia kaoi" ("Go back, go back, I go onwards"). Boobardy turned to retrace his steps and on looking backward he saw that the tree had vanished in a cloud of smoke. This beautiful tree is now the Southern Cross and the stars the notches whereby the spirits of the dead climb to Bhaiame. Notches on a tree are also pointed out as Mundowa.

This, briefly, is the Aboriginal story of the creation and how man was bought into the world."[25]

Figure 34: Mount Yengo[26]

Having concluded this interpretation, Slater would have immediately realised, as we did, that this appearance of an exclusive right foot imprint, totally lacking in any hint of a corresponding left-foot makes it compulsory that the "nameless one"[27] does indeed have a name, and it has to be Baiame. We know as an absolute rule that whenever just a right-foot imprint is engraved in the rock throughout not just the Wollombi, but anywhere on this continent, this must be Baiame's business.

It is for this reason that Slater supplied a more detailed and nuanced description of what just the right-foot alone must mean. "Bhaiame, which means, "Cut off to build," apparently cut off one of his legs in order to make the man Boobardy (meaning Father: the Father of Mankind), and making him in his own image, left him one leg only. That is why a single footprint is called Mundowa."[28]

That Baiame refused to eat meat may seem somewhat perplexing in a country of hunter-gatherers but strangely enough that concept of being vegetarian has turned up elsewhere in Dreaming Stories. So too, the fact that Boobardy left the Nameless One expecting him to die is somewhat contradictory because further on he returns and tracks him while professing a desire to follow his footsteps. There is an inherent contradiction in his actions simply because after eschewing a diet of meat, Boobardy is now prepared to wander off into constellations with him.

And it is that central theme of the interconnection of 'as on top' to this terrestrial tale, that is dominant at Burragurra. Slater added at the end of his explanation the main reason why the nameless one had to be Baiame declaring that "the disappearance of the Mundowa footprints is also explained in the story written on the rocks. He brought living things from on high and then stepped back into the high regions from whence he came."[29]

The Female Blanks and Omissions

What also warrants further consideration was that the "men"[30] were placed into a "deep sleep,"[31] but the woman was not. We can only assume that she remained awake while the men slept for a considerable time, but this void seems to be the norm in this ancient creation myth. Slater also concedes that "in the story of the creation no mention is made of the method adopted by Bhaiame in the making of Numbardy (mother), who, as the wife of Turramullan, was called Muni Burre-bean (giving life with breasts). But as Mulla Mulla, wife of Wabooee (another name for Turramullan, whose name was not allowed to be mentioned outside the sacred circle), it appears from her name that she was lifted down alive from a high place, and so, instead of being made on earth, she came from the sky above, where Bhaiame dwells."[32]

This is not a metaphor or allegory, it means both the male and female creation beings were never from this rock planet, anywhere else other than Earth is possible, but as to being born on Earth, for both that is definite no-show, it just didn't happen here. Outside women having breasts this male Dreaming story has nothing-which from any Original male perspective this is to be expected. Such serious women's business should never be mentioned in men's business. The only thing they actually share is not being born on this planet, but as to what happened next well there are two stories, and we only have the male side of the events.

What does resonate is an underlying Gnostic theme of free-falling arrogance, when Yaltaboath[33], the first creation of the Supreme God, does not recognise anyone before himself and allows his eyes and ego to fill in the gaps.

Figure 35: Yaldabaoth[34]

No Mouth

Boobardy is wearing "hat"[35]/helmet, so too is Bulgandry, as are many other engraved Sky Heroes, and none of them, just like the Wandjina[36] figures of the Kimberleys[37], have any form of a mouth. And it is that deliberate omission that sets the entire esoteric scenery not just at Burragurra but throughout the Wollombi and Gosford.

Figure 36: The Wandjina[38]

Professor Elkin, who was the first Professor of the very first Anthropological Faculty at Sydney University and has never had his credentials questioned, declared that the engravings at the Wollombi and Gosford region "definitely"[39] have a "religious function."[40] What he saw as "the principal motive"[41] in reaching that conclusion was "a head with eyes and nose, but no mouth representing the principle of life." [42]

Chapter 8

"SYMBOLIC WRITING" BY FREDERIC SLATER

"It will be necessary to invent a new word to explain what these rock carvings really are. One is apt to be misunderstood when calling them picture words for immediately there arises in the mind's eye the Egyptian Hieroglyphics – and the most ancient form of the alphabet – and there is a demand for an associated word. It will be found later on in the "Book of Translations" and the "Book of Searchings" that many of the symbols on these rocks were the origin of Egyptian Hieroglyphics and bear the same meaning. I prefer to call them picture language using the word just as one refers to an engraving on which a cutting medium or implement has been used and not a brush. At the same time they come under the comprehensive term ideograph, because they present to the eye the idea which could not be conveyed in written words, an alphabet not having been developed when they were originated. They were on their way some of the symbols which are on these rock pictures have found a place in the alphabets at present in use. Anthropological and archaeological researchers, particularly Egyptologists, will find nothing startling in a statement of this kind. In a measure they anticipate things and are able to visualise what is coming.

The common origin of humanity is an established fact. What we are seeing is the centre from whence the human family emanated in the beginning of human life, when this particular part of the primordial family – the Australian Aborigines – arrived in the land [sic] and how they got there. The records which we have found on the rocks establishes their Nilotic origin and the fact they were food gatherers in the beginning and remain food gatherers to this day shows that their ancestors began the great trek before agriculture was invented. Opinions of the time vary on this point. Petrie says that agriculture was invented 11,00 years ago. But the first exodus took place 300,000 years ago or more. The so called Aboriginals of Australia are of a type of a later exodus. The date would be nearer 100,000 years ago instead of 10,000. It is for evidence of this that we have to look in the picture records and ideographs they have left us and in the language which they still speak.

Similar picture records to those found in Australia have been found in other parts of the world. Their interpretation has so far defied the probing of researchers because they find no keys to unlock the secrets. An exception might be taken with regard to that master prober Dr. Albert Churchward who has unravelled many of the stories and who will find in these pictures much that he has, in a measure, anticipated. The reason that they have escaped interpretation by many scholarly men who have attempted to read them is because they have taken too scholarly a course. In other words they have used keys for complicated locks to open a door that was closed with a simple belt. These records are hidden deep under chambers of residence, of many families who have marched along the highways of time – submerged under languages that again have been submerged until the records become a riddle. Not so in Australia. The syllabic language which they brought with them to Australia can be reconstructed, or revocalised, from the many dialects into which it has been split and built upon. It has been preserved to a great extent in the ceremonial ritual and ethical teachings and is here inscribed on the rocks in picture language.

Knowing the history, to say nothing about the philosophy and the language, some of which is written in figures, (linear writing is the oldest form of writing) I venture the opinion that the chief characteristic in the primordial age which distinguish man from the rest of creation was his power of speech. I am drawn towards this conclusion by the manner of their second method of writing. The first figures with the words for the elementary powers being in strokes with the exception of 10 (Thoorale-moori) which is represented by a U (reversed). Whilst their additional method was with dots inside a circle or their hieroglyphic-like symbol which has become the Greek letter Omega by means of which they delineated the senses, the head itself being the ideograph for the power of speech. The word for speech "Ghungaw" (Gu-no-goa) – the head – meaning "I speak for all". A representation of a dead person was a body without a head. The power to communicate by means of speech was inherent in man from the dawn of creation. With this speech of syllabic words there came the added interpretation in signs, gesture and motion with the still further additional power to draw pictures to make himself understood. All these methods of reaching the understanding wee used by the Aboriginals in connection with the ceremonies recorded in these pictures. All writing is symbolical. Every letter of every alphabet is an ideograph.

The best exposition of what an ideograph really is can be found in our everyday reading of newspapers and in the everyday work of professional people. Here are some ideographs that will be readily recognised. They are not words, they are signs that represent ideas, immediately creating a mental picture:

$X \; + \; = \; £ \; / \; \div \; \sqrt{}$

As a matter of fact our language which is fast becoming unwieldly with its preponderance is returning to symbolical form: S.O.S. , E. & O.E., C.O.D. , F.O.B. , F.A.Q. , St. , A.N.Z.A.C. and so forth. You can multiply them at your will. They do not spell a word. They are ideographs that represent ideas.

Forms of writing, like language – and one should add spelling – change so quickly that the writing of a century ago presents difficulties to most people. Ten steppingstones of the average family life take one back to the Elizabethan Age when the most glorious page of our literary history was inscribed in letters of gold, when our ancestors could have walked and talked with Shakespeare. Yet today there is a loud lament that so little of Shakespeare's handwriting has been left. Shakespeare's handwriting was in the old style which had been taught by Walter Roche, a man of learning and importance, whose influence kept Shakespeare from pursuing the new form of writing which was the pride of every schoolboy in London at that time. I doubt if a play of Shakespeare's written in his own handwriting could be read off hand by one in a million people. And I doubt if the handwriting of a great man of today, dictating a few hundred words daily to stenographers and typists, will be found 300 years hence. Shakespeare's work lives in the ideographs of the scribes not in the ideographs of his own handwriting. Shakespeare's words live translated into the ideographs of our time and should a work of his be found written in the manner he was taught to write, it could be interpreted by comparison with the words of the printed book. In the same way the language of the Australian Aboriginals lives and, with the aid of the ideographs, the story can be read.

Britain, with all its scholarliness and its Latin scholars from Julius Caesar onward to the year 407 has no written language. Its people were dependent upon picture writing and Druidical symbols brought from Egypt together with a peculiar linear writing. At no greater a distance than 1530 years the people were no further advanced than Australia's Aboriginals. They had a strange alphabet called Ogam which very much resembles the Aborigines method of linear numeration. There is little doubt that it originated from the primordial method. This form of writing was used in Britain, Scotland and Ireland less than 450 years before Shakespeare was born. Yet there are no more than 300 examples in existence. It shows, however, that the civilisations of today are but a span compared with the time when primordial man first arrived in Australia and he has left relics in the shape of ideographs which are of great importance and which are just as easy to read.

The intellectual backwardness of Australia's Aborigines is said to be illustrated by their method of counting, using their fingers and toes. This method of counting still survives. In England the tally stick was used until 1826 to keep accounts in the exchequer in the palace of Westminster. This method of keeping accounts was introduced in the days of Canute who died in 1033. When the tally stick system was abolished the burning of sticks in the stoves of the House of Lords caused the fire which burnt down the Houses of Parliament. That was only 111 years ago. Yet with all its knowledge and learning the British race left few decipherable records even on its tally sticks. Whereas Australia's Aboriginals in notch figures tell a story of more than 100,000 years ago and in such notches can be found the beginning of the great arithmetical age. Their ten figures or ten fingers, have never been improved upon. We still have to double ten if we wish to express the double number.

The Australian Aboriginal's ideographs gave the bases of the alphabet in which we formulate our words today. They were the germ of the Egyptian Hieroglyphics which were borrowed from the ideographs of the remote ancestors of Australia's Aboriginals. They are not difficult to read if one gets back to the root word of the language – the syllabic language – I call it the spiritual language in which these words were made pictorially more than a hundred years ago. Possibly it is the original language of man.

Though the language of the Australian Aborigines is broken up into many dialects, it is still a unity. It has a root origin which when vocalised makes it understandable. It is still syllabic, every syllable having a vowel ending. In its proper vocalisation it is mellifluous, rhythmic and capable of wonderful expressiveness. Words are strung together like links in a chain or bells of different notes on a string. Break a word into syllables and each syllable tells a story, or builds up a story. I best illustrate this by taking a word that almost everyone has heard: Mundowa. It is a name given throughout the length and breadth of Australia to certain footprints carved on rocks, impressed in clay or painted in caves. It is also applied to certain notches chopped in tree trunks with the aid of which Aboriginals are able to climb to a great height. Ask an Aboriginal what he calls them and he will say "Foot make 'em mark." But the word for the ordinary footprint is curriaree (soles of the feet). What appears to be an evasive answer is not to be wondered at.

Apart from the fact that few present day Aboriginals living close to populated places do not know the meaning of these rock carvings, which date back in their original form tens of thousands of years, the initiate when viewing the mysteries for the first time has to swear and oath not to reveal what has been seen or heard. The oath of obedience expressed in song is solemnly chanted not once but many times until the drone of it and the importance of it goes into the initiate's brain. I doubt if a correct version of the meaning of these rock carvings can be obtained outside the tribes who still live in a primitive state. Something will either be evaded or the one questioned will take the ideas from the questioner. To illustrate what I mean I will take the word Parramatta, the name of the first town outside of Sydney after the landing of the settlers who accompanied Governor Phillip. This word for 150 years has been interpreted "Eels sit down here." The meaning of it is "Dark Scrub" or "Jungle" referring to the mangroves which line the river banks where "the eels sat down" of course. "Parra" means "dark" or "night" and "matta" "scrub" (close growing stunted trees or brushwood). For instance the name given by the natives to the South Head light house was "Parrawee" meaning "The Night Light" (or "fire").

One can imagine how this oath was impressed on the initiate. A figure with "many eyes" confronted the youth. The oath he was taking was chanted all round him. There was the light of fires, the clash of weapons and the beating of waddies and the thud of feet giving time and motion to the song as the Elders danced round the initiate. The sight of the "many-eyed" figures peeping through the bushes from behind from whom came the swirling sound of the bull roarers was enough to cause a youth to be impressed. No wonder the meaning of Mundowa has remained a secret.

In the word Mundowa is the story of the genesis of man: "He who came from on high brought living things (or life) into the world." In other words "God has walked here." He was known as "Muun" ("The Giver of life"). It was a blasphemy to mention his name, except within the area of ceremony. He is never represented except in footprints.

This symbol of the foot and the genesis of man corresponds with the most ancient records."[1]

Chapter 9

THE DATE WOULD BE NEARER TO 100,000 YEARS

To even suggest any date past 20,000 years as the maximum date of Original presence in Australia in the 1930's is a huge call, and increasing the numbers by a factor of five is really pushing the boundaries, and still is today. Yes, elsewhere in his book Slater has also thrown in even larger numbers into this equation, he has also suggested 150,000, 250,000 and 300,000 years as being appropriate. There seems to be an inconsistency here as the time span he gives spreads over 150,000 years, but it needs to be appreciated there was no technology then that could supply such numbers and these approximations are educated guesses by Slater.

The point being when it comes to hundreds of thousands, such numbers are not in any Original vocabulary or numerology, but when it comes to Australian archaeology such numbers are immediately dismissed as fictional. Mainstream academia claims that before 60,000 years there was no-one in Australia bar the kangaroos and an assortment of marsupials.

The Real Facts and Unreal Rebuttals

We will open this very brief examination of eight Australian sites and human bones by first listing the dates calculated by scientists of unchallenged pedigree. The list could be much larger, but these locations are sufficient in making an unchallengeable point of contention, and include Point Ritchie 120,000 years, Great Barrier Reef[1] 180,000 years, Lake George[2] 120,000 years, Panaramitee[3] >75,000 years, Jinmium[4] 116-176,000 years and a collection of robust skulls found at Lake Mungo[5], Kow Swamp[6] and Cossack[7] dated between 50-6,000 years. In each case the supporting science is solid, and because of inconvenience of the sites, in every verdict alternative explanations, often based on extremely tenuous verging on ridiculous assumptions, have been readily given and eagerly endorsed. The point that needs to be made is that if only one of these dates is actually correct then the Out-of-Africa theory espousing African Homo sapien sapiens arriving in Australia between 50-60,000 years ago is wrong.

LOCATION	ACTIVITY	DATE
Great Barrier Reef	Fire-Stick Farming	186,000
Jinmium	Tools	176,000
Lake Eyre	Skullcap	135,000
Lake George	Fire-Stick Farming	120,000
Devonport	Rock-engraving	> 115,000
Jinmium	Art	75,000 -116,000
Point Richie	Shell Middens	120,000
Panaramittee	Rock-engraving of saltwater Crocodile	75,000
Rottnest Island	Tools	70,000
Lake Mungo	WHL 3 Complete Skeleton	61,000 - 65,000
Lake Mungo	WHL 1 Cremated Bones	61,000

Figure 37: Eleven Sites with Anomalous Dates[8]

Jim Bowler[9] has been until very recently a staunch defender of the traditionally accepted Out-of-Africa theory, and even when initially announcing a date of no less than 90,000 years for the archaeology found at Moyjil (Point Richie, Victoria) he equivocated. He stood by the science used to calculate this date, but knowing the implications of that date, stated that he needed more confirmation. Which is exactly what happened, and what made this site even more inconvenient at every academic level was that the dates returned were 30,000 years older, he was now defending a date of no less than 120,000 years. He openly conceded this was not going to be accepted, but he felt he had no choice but to do good science and endorse their findings.

What they had was a copious amount of charcoal found at a site resembling a fire-place/hearth, and a sizeable midden of shells deposited on the beach. Those who could not bring themselves to accept such a revision responded with two alternatives that have no base in precedent or fact. Firstly, the charcoal was due to a bushfire. How such an intense fire could be present on the sand by the seaside is nigh on impossible to envisage. During the last intense bush fire season, and many before, as the fires neared towns and settlements those fleeing always made it to the beaches for safety, there has never been one instance where any fire spread to the sand, not ever.

No less ridiculous was the explanation tended that the clustering of seashells in middens was not due to human activity but through the actions of sea gulls with a communal mind-set. It was postulated that the sea gulls gathered the shells from various locations and then carried them to one common dining area then ate and carefully deposited the discarded shells in one specific spot. They gave no example of this happening anywhere before or now, nor did they cite the studies of any scientists observing such activities. But simply because there was no other viable explanation, except the obvious, they were compelled to invent a fictional narrative.

Understandably Bowler has rejected both unscientific alternatives and relied solely on good science with lashings of pure common sense. He openly admits many will find his current research unpalatable, but did warn them their research is ongoing and he expects there will be more dates in six-figures on the horizon. He knows, as we do, that the accepted notion of Africans arriving at the very top of northern Australia, then slowly edging along the coastline and taking at least 20-30,000 years to reach the far southern extremities of Australia, which is where Point Ritchie is located, leads to a first entry date of no less than 150,000 years. Such mathematics seriously challenges every aspect of the Out-of-Africa theory. Nonetheless, that is what his science unequivocally states as fact, and is what Slater knows not to be true.

Déjà vu

Within a second of first reading Bowler's hedged proviso, that he needed confirmation through other dates and preferably elsewhere that returned similar figures, I immediately thought back to the work that he, along with Gurdup Singh[10] and Peter Ouwendyke did in 1982 at the Great Barrier Reef.[11] They did some core sampling on the reef that stretched back millions of years, and noticed a massive increase in charcoal beginning at around 180,000 years ago.

All of the archaeologists involved released a joint statement justifying both the science behind this announcement and the reasons why they believed this was tangible proof of human activity. They understandably came to the conclusion that this was evidence of fire-stick farming, and that Original humans were responsible. They ruled out massive changes in climate, or other potential causes and focused on the real possibility that humans were lighting fires. They clearly knew that such a date being announced in 1982 was guaranteed to be slated, criticised and ridiculed, but were convinced the science was sound and that no other option was 'left on the table.'

It is not as if they were amateurs or unqualified, in fact Gurdup Singh was Australia's expert in core sampling and had already intensively examined numerous other sites in Australia. What I did find somewhat perplexing is that Bowler was having an 'each-way' bet in stating the science is good but because the date was so large, he wanted the same numbers on other sites, but he already had that confirmation at the Great Barrier Reef. Moreover, as Singh had already announced that the numbers coming out of his sampling at Lake George were in six-figures, and Bowler surely knew this, his equivocation just didn't make sense. Well, knowing how conservative Australian archaeology was then, and still is, we do understand why Bowler was so hesitant, but regardless the science used at Lake George was identical to that at the reef and both numbers totally discounted any form of the Out-of-Africa theory.

Lake George

At Lake George Singh drilled down to a level that equated to four million years, and at this location he noticed the same huge spike in charcoal accumulation beginning at 128,000 years. He looked further and deeper and found that most dramatic spikes in charcoal corresponded to periods of high lake levels. Which meant the increase in fire activity took place not during drier periods but when moisture levels were high. Logically this rules out the main natural cause of bush fires through drought.

Singh also knew that because this southern site is so far from the coast, if humans first came from Africa and first occupied the northern areas, it would take no less than twenty thousand years before first reaching such locations. Despite this major hurdle he persisted simply because he was the expert in such archaeological pursuits and science, what he did was the best there was.

However, one scientist just had to find something to question, and Richard Wright[12] objected claiming a date of 60,000 years is applicable. Many academics immediately agreed, but that is contradictory from every Out-of-Africa perspective, simply because we have to add no less than 20,000 years to this number and an entry date from Africa of over 80,000 years is a very uncomfortable fit. And in what only adds to the discomfort of Wright's much more conservative calculations, is another date coming out of archaeology that is further south and further inland.

Figure 38: Lake George[13]

Panaramitee

The best way to introduce the antiquity or uncomfortable numbers of this engraving on rock is to open with a quote from the highly respected Australian archaeologist, Josephine Flood[14]. She was quite taken by the science of the Panaramitee engraving of a salt-water crocodile, in particular its size and location created all manner of contradictions.

"I am going to be so bold as to suggest that it may derive from a time when terrestrial crocodiles and humans co-existed in South Australia, although the youngest crocodiles found so far date to more than 75,000 years at Cuddie Springs."[15] She is absolutely correct in supplying a minimum age of 75,000 years, as it has been a considerable time since salt-water crocodiles with a head of over two metres in length were swimming in any desert tribal estates in that area. She openly concedes this engraved crocodile "has always been an enigma",[16] but because "of the thick layer of desert varnish on the petroglyph"[17] she felt that date was logical and consistent with the fauna, geology and climate of this area. In saying this, Flood knows that the date she was so "bold"[18] to suggest, of itself calls into question all versions of the Out-of-Africa theory, however, it is entirely consistent with Slater's collection of six-figured Australian dates.

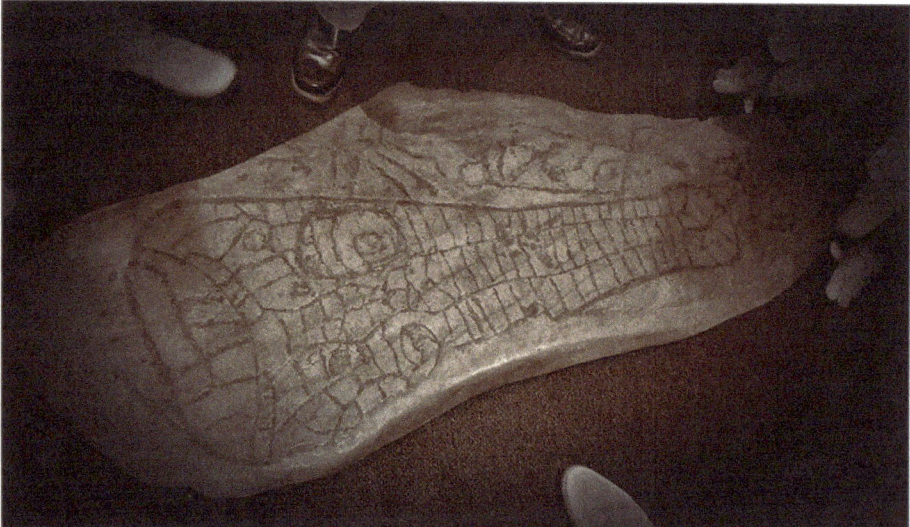

Figure 39: Replica of Panaramitee Crocodile Engraving[19]

"Jinmium-Oldest one day, Youngest the Next"

"An antiquity was alleged of between 116 000 and 176 000 years for Aboriginal stone tools and between 75 000 and 116 000 years for artistic activity inferred from ochre in Jinmium rockshelter in the Keep River area of the Northern Territory."[20] These incredibly radical dates caused a lot of resentment, the problem being that the three authors, Professor Richard Fullagar[21], David Price[22] and Professor Lesley Head[23] all of Wollongong University, have the very best credentials and relied on the highly regarded dating process of thermoluminescence. This paper, as controversial as it was, did get published in the premier academic journal Antiquity in December 1996.[24]

Within two months of publication there were two opposing papers written by a total of thirteen academics, and the reports of these articles in dispute concluded that together they "convincingly challenged"[25] the findings of the offending three. Careful not to sully their colleagues' expertise, they did "suggest"[26] an alternative that seemed utterly impossible to authenticate. They did not challenge the credentials of either the academics or the rigour of their science, but found a path of least offence in suggesting "that some grains have older optical ages because they received insufficient exposure to sunlight before burial. The presence of such grains in a sample will cause age overestimates using multiple-grain methods, whether using thermoluminescence or optical dating."[27]

How can anyone who does not attend a funeral or burial accurately declare where the burial was, or that the rock or person was in the shade or in full sunlight? It is a totally unverifiable hypothesis, and certainly nowhere near "convincingly"[28] conclusive. Anyone claiming to know where a rock was originally 10,000 years ago is clutching at straws, whether there are one or thirteen people clutching is irrelevant. At best it is a 50/50 proposition, but when placed in context with the other four sites previously briefly discussed, the chances increase that another six figures, which is very much in keeping with Slater's mathematics, is just 'par for the Australian course.'

What if the Nay-sayers are Correct four Times Over?

These huge numbers are correct, but for the sake of looking at every angle, even if the critics are correct in their dismissals, there is another site they have all authenticated that conclusively dismisses any external input of modern gracile African Homo sapien sapiens ever coming to Australia irrespective of dates and sequences claimed.

This undeniable Out-of-Africa rebuttal begins at Lake Mungo, and has nothing to do with the two gracile remains of Mungo 1[29] and 3[30]. Arguments about whether a date of 40 or 60,000 years old are still current, but what has not been understood or appreciated is what the fiftieth set of skulls and bones recovered mean because of their extremely unique physiology, and in particular, bone thickness.

Figure 40: Lake Mungo[31]

The official reports describing this extremely robust individual (WLH 50[32]) were no less than sensational and often much more. It was observed that "WLH 50 is massive: he is so robust."[33] There were so many things about this skull that had no equivalent, anywhere or at any time. "The cranium is extremely wide and approximately 210 millimetres"[34] and "the cranial vault bone averages 16 millimetres thick."[35] The face is markedly different from any other hominid with "massive brow ridges forming a continuous torus above the eyes"[36] and a forehead that is virtually missing, being so "flat and receding."[37] When it comes to the skull's shape everything is on a non-hominid tangent, it "is flask-shaped,"[38] "extremely wide"[39] and "the greatest width occurs very low in back view."[40] When throwing into this package the facial features of bone and flesh that many may construe to be primitive in appearance, nothing could be further from the truth.

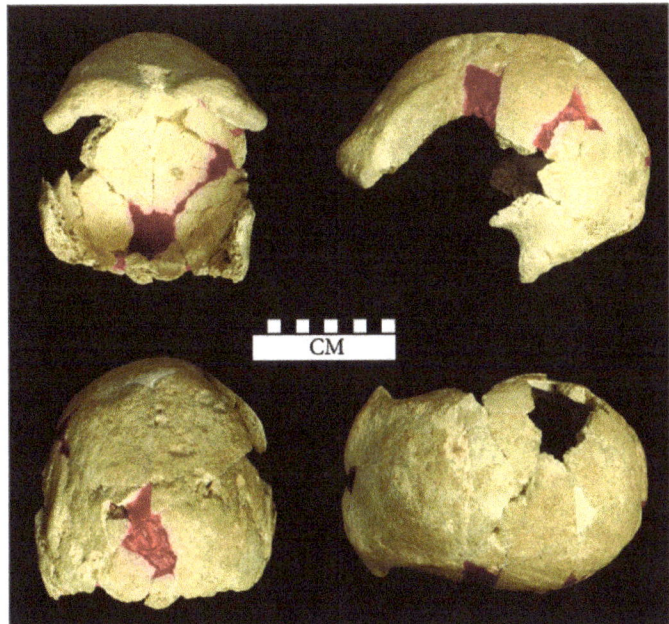

Figure 41: WLH 50 Skullcap[41]

What astounded the researchers was not just that it had the thickest skull ever, so too was its actual volume unprecedented. Modern humans have an average endocranial volume of 1300 millilitres, but WLH 50 had reading of 1540 millilitres. If this is an actual scientific fact, which it is, it seems rational to observe that if this being is much stronger, powerful and far more intelligent, the questions about how or if it is related to sapiens or hominids arises. Especially since "his body was equally massive"[42] with his "elbow bone" being "enormous."[43] The multiplicity of issues relating to these people being in anyway genetically related to the supposed arrival and continental settlement by the gracile sapien beings spill out all over the countryside.

All that left before assembling any sensible response is to factor in the timing. The agreed age is "more probably in excess of 40,000 to 50,000 years"[44] and was calculated "by John Head of the Radiocarbon Dating Research Unit of the Australian National University."[45] Such a date brings us right back to the supposed first arrival date of between 50 to 60,000 years, and Alan Thorne[46] is absolutely right in declaring that "robust WLH 50 could not possibly be descended from the gracile type of WLH 1."[47] The inescapable reason why there can be no genetic interaction is all about skull thickness, it comes down to the numbers and ratios when in comparison. WLH 1 has a skull that is between 1-2 millimetres thick, while WLH 50 has a skull thickness that varies between 15-19 millimetres. Josephine Flood succinctly highlighted how clearly different the genetic ancestry of the robust and gracile beings were in observing that the contrast in thickness of the skulls "is as great as that between earthenware and bone china, or an orange peel and eggshell."[48]

Figure 42: Mungo Man[49]

That discrepancy in the thickness of bone can add up to an increase in percentage of 1,900%. This robust skull is 15.6% larger and 31.6% wider, but looks so primitive. Nevertheless, it just isn't a primitive dull relic from the past. One of the most eminent anthropologists in the world, Professor Chris Stringer[50], examined and measured WLH 50 and was positive that this skull is "anatomically modern rather than archaic."[51]

Call it a Mutation and Look the Other way.

If I had to sum up what the long-term outcome and impact of WLH 50's appearance has been in academic and official circles, it was to simply call it a mutation yet offer no science or precedent and once done, look the other way and say no more. No this is not part of a Monty Python script, but the Australian scientific mantra of not only yesterday, but tomorrow.

The problem being as much as the authorities hoped this robust hurdle would just go away, not long after it came back, but it wasn't one more inconvenient appearance, but no less than forty individuals were found. Everything seen and measured on that one robust skull at Lake Mungo was multiplied forty times over at Kow Swamp (inland Northern Victoria). Just as it was at Lake Mungo all of these remains had "prominent brow ridges and flat, receding foreheads."[52] What was found just did not fit into every current theory about human presence in Australia, "the jaws and teeth are huge, indeed some mandibles are more massive than those of Java Man."[53]

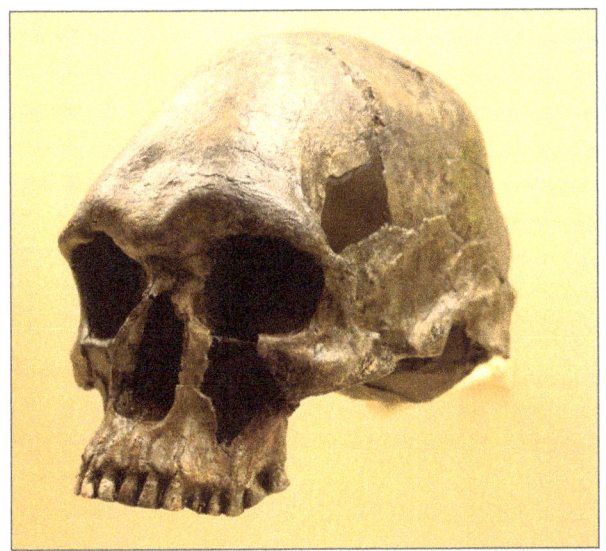

Figure 43: Kow Swamp 1[54]

It was relatively easy to ignore or provide some very tenuous alternative explanations for one solitary skull, but this discovery demanded a more substantial response. "The skeletons found at Kow Swamp included men, women, juveniles and infants. The burial complex is at present the largest single population of the late Pleistocene epoch found in one locality anywhere in the world. Kow Swamp is thus of great importance not only for Australia, but also for world prehistory."[55]

Because of these undeniable imperatives the officials had no option but to look, examine, then misplace all forty sets of bones and skulls forever. And that is exactly what they did, after all the preliminary investigation was completed, everything was 'lost.' The Government does not dispute that they removed then examined, but as to what happened next, it is all a mystery. One the foremost world anthropologists, Chris Stringer, called what took place next to be the greatest archaeological crime of the twentieth century, and he is undeniably right, "when the remains were returned, they were destroyed by the traditional descendants. This was a "great loss to science and to the human race as a whole"".[56] Stringer goes on to say, "I am not saying all of it [the material] has been destroyed ... but certainly I don't see it being available for scientific study,"[57] While Professor Robert Foley[58] of Cambridge University summarises this situation as "It seems to me there is a danger that the whole continent of Australia will be out of bounds for research into the origins of those people ... What we are concerned about is that the working group will come up with a simple, blanket solution for some very complex issues."[59] The official explanation is that the government allege they returned all the bones to the local Lands Council for interment, and the Lands Council reject this claim insisting that did not happen. The only truth remaining is that all forty skulls and bones are still missing in inaction.

What is intriguing and incredibly suspicious is that soon after the skulls went 'walkabout,' the government constructed a huge rectangular three-metre earthen wall around Kow Swamp then flooded the entire swamp. No more archaeology has been conducted and what is intriguing is that Kow Swamp is in a very low-rainfall location yet not one drop of the stored reservoir of water has ever been used for irrigation, it just sits there. They destroyed the site and not a word of protest or dissension was heard, which means the same site is of no importance beyond being a stagnant massive pool of water.

Just when those who decide felt they had finally dealt with the pesky robust issue, soon after another robust skull was found at Cossack (Western Australia) and it was dated at 6,000 years. And what was even more unwelcome was that "Cossack Man has the most sloping forehead and is the most long-headed (dolichocephalic) Aborigine yet found in past or present Australia."[60] The recuring point of contention is that all Out-of-Africa theories have an African crew that is solely gracile, and as Alan Thorne correctly observed, this modern robust species is not related.

So, irrespective of whatever denials and ridiculous alternatives offered in discounting the cluster of dates exceeding any proposed entry of African graciles, none of that explains why there is another race of hominids, deemed to be fully modern, in Australia for at least over forty thousand years. Then throw in the Australian little people we have discussed often, then the Yowies[61] that are on our rain-forest property and the whole assemblage means that any allegation that all bipedal beings in this country are sourced from boat voyage of a few African gracile Homo sapien sapiens is null and void. That just isn't true, and as for the date of first settlement, Slater is on the right track, but the dates are even older, much older, as they were always here to begin with.

Words and Pictures

Slater never varies in his description on the very First Language in being a global form of communication that relies on picture words. He does equivocate in his comparisons to one of its later off-shoots, Egyptian hieroglyphs, as he feels it is too restrictive in content. From his understanding these pictures are more ideographs in that they represent concepts, and this extends even further in a land where the principal form of communication is oral. Many of these symbols have attached to them Dreaming Stories, ceremonies and rituals.

He believes every spoken language on this planet, past and present, has its origins in Australia. "The common origin of humanity is an established fact, what we are seeing is the centre from whence the human family emanated in the beginning."[62] And it is in Australia that enough remains to trace back to the very beginning. The reason why Slater can be so bold, is not just because he had access to the Great Record Book compiled by Dunlop, but it is equally due to the fundamental mistake the archaeologists and linguists have made from their first attempts to interpret. He is adamant they "have taken a too scholarly course. In other words, they have used keys for complicated locks to open a door that was closed by a belt."[63]

At this stage of proceedings, there is a need to substantiate this premise of all languages being sourced from Australia. An extremely easy task, so much so that we will have to pick and choose, but to begin with we will first examine the research of Dr. Hermann Klaatsch[64]. Professor Klaatsch was trying to convince German and European academics that intensive field studies was the path that all archaeologists and anthropologists should take and employ as the first measure. He spent four years in Australia (1904-1907) exclusively studying Original Old Way tribal customs, ceremonies, beliefs and what was his personal first choice, language.

He believed, as did Slater, that Original languages were the mother-tongue for all other languages, it only took days on site before the semantic similarities became evident and from that point on it never stopped. Klaatsch's methodology was sound, he sought out the most elemental notions and words from ancient European and Asian languages and then tried to find within Original languages similar words. And in that respect the comparisons all told one story and came from the same source.

"The Australian dialects seem in many respects to be fragments of the primitive speech of man. The words which are the same over considerable regions or found with the same meaning in widely distant localities have the best right to be considered primitive, and it is precisely amongst that we find the most striking resemblances to Indo-German words. The word "manda" (= hand), for instance, is found over a large area, and recalls the Latin manus (and the English and German "hand"). In the word "mera" (compare "woomera," the original of "boomerang") or "mara" we see some affinity to the Greek meros (= member). Not less striking is the resemblance of "bina" (ear, leaf, feather, etc) to the corresponding Latin word pinna. In Queensland I found the word "jepar" for "liver," which is in Greek "hepar"; and Basedow, an authority on the Australians, gives "kapata" for "head" (Latin caput) as used by a central Australian tribe. There is a flourishing little town in New South Wales"[65] (sic, it is just over the border in Queensland) "called Toowoomba (or Tuwumba) after a "cucumber" (Latin cucumba) that grows in the district."[66] "The Latin acqua, the English "water" (British and irish "usk," German "wasser,"etc.), which remind us of the constantly repeated "arra," "warra" and "larra" of the Australian dialects."[67]

Figure 44: Professor / M.D. Hermann Klaatsch[68]

There are many more pages of Klaatsch's book devoted to the semantic similarities originating in Australia. So much so that Klaatsch intentionally highlighted how strong the connection of languages was by somewhat patronisingly presenting one explanation given to him as to why all ancient languages have an Australian heritage. He did this solely to emphasise how interconnected everything was to Australia, but we suspect it was given with an accompanying snigger. "We can quite understand how the missionaries who studied the language in the early days of colonisation were led by the many resemblances to words of the "Indo-Germanic" group to believe that the aboriginals (sic) had once lived at a more advanced level of culture; though of this there is no question. According to the missionaries it was the confusion of tongues at the tower of Babel that cut off the ancestors of the Australians from other races. Childish as these ideas are, they are of value in some respects, as they give us an impartial testimony to the Indo-Germanic affinities of the Australians."[69]

Irrespective of how much of Klaatsch's observations we include some will find a way of discrediting or demanding more proof, and to that end we feel a closer look at the 'Indo' half of this linguistic relationship will assist in defining where and possibly appease the hard-core doubters. In the Southern section of India "the Dravidian fishermen of the Madras coast use almost the same words for *I, thou, he, we* and *you* as some Aboriginal tribes. All the Dravidian dialects are agglutinative, as are Australian languages. Australian canoes are constructed identically to those of the Dravidian tribes, and wild tribes in the Deccan region of India are the only culture known to use the boomerang outside Australia (with the possible exception of ancient Egypt)."[70]

The Last Word

Until my 'boss Elder' Karno sent me a sheet of paper he called "Possum Dreaming" there was still an element of maybe lurking in the background. Initially I had no idea what it meant or even why Karno sent this one sheet of paper with 27 symbols marked out by him. But what did intrigue me was the blue outer and inner circle of symbols were of "Githubal" origin, and more to the point, he is not Githubal[71] and that tribal estate is over three thousands kilometres to the south-west from his Ramindjeri tribal lands.

More importantly is the incontestable fact that he has never seen any of eighteen letters Slater wrote relating to the Standing Stones site. Therefore, the fact that all of the fifteen Githubal picturegrams Karno sent me are also in Slater's notes written in 1939, defies every rational explanation. They are identical, exactly the same. Slater claimed that the Githubal symbols are part of the very first language, Karno made the same claim in 2014 and proved it. There is no explanation other than both men were writing from the same ancient script. No-one could ever challenge Karno when it comes to Old Way Original cultural matters, and Karno's confirmation really does conclude the need to go any further.

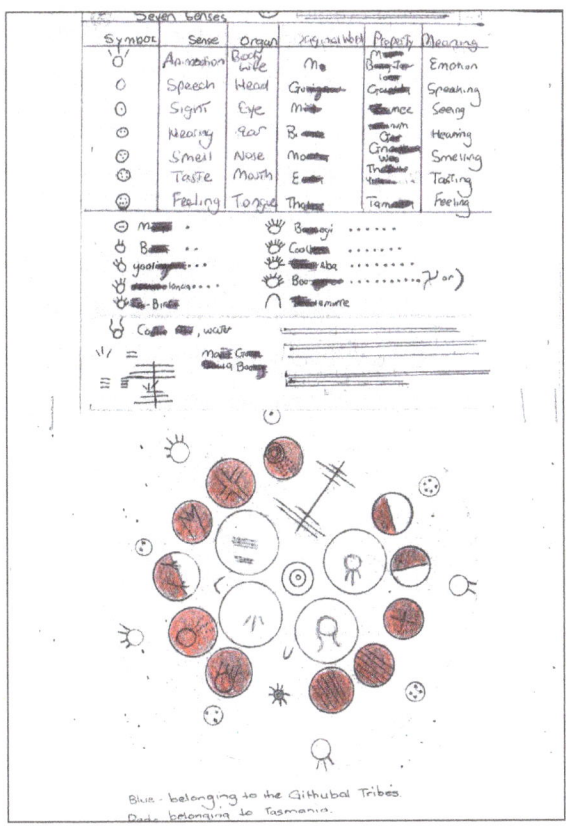

Figure 45: Possum Dreaming- Mix of Karno's & Slater's Symbols[72]

Chapter 10

"STONE AGE AUTHORS" BY FREDERIC SLATER

"This translation of the ideographs and writing together with the hieroglyphs by the Stone-Age authors is based on an original investigation of the Aboriginal language spoken in the district where the rock carvings were first discovered. The Aboriginals never use two words where one will do. They roll several words into one by clipping off and combining potions of words. Other words are detached from phrases and from sentences. A not uncommon custom. Their meaning is quite clear when detached words are supplied. The language, with many variations due to neighbouring dialectic changes, has an affinity with Kamilaroi [sic-Gumilaroi], a very compact vocabulary which has been published by Rev. William Ridley, B. A. (London) and M.A. (Sydney) under the tribal title. The book was printed by the New South Wales Government Printer in 1875. This affinity accounts for the statement that the Kamilaroi [sic] language was familiar to all Aboriginals. My chief source of assistance in investigation however, has been an unpublished manuscript of the sacred language as spoken around the Wollombi (where there is also a dialect) collected by Mrs. David Dunlop [sic] which she calls "Murree Gwalda, or the Blacks' Language of the Comileroi." "Murree Gwalda" really means "The Soul" or the "Spirit" language; or the language which has brought the light of God to the earth. Perhaps the phrase as the Aboriginals understood it should be "The language which God gave to man when light dawned on the earth." It is expressed in the hieroglyph which is at Burragurra and Yango and was one of the first names of Egypt. IAU (the "Light of the World") more often called "The Son of Light."

    According to the notes left by Mrs. Dunlop Comileroi was variously pronounced in different areas; but was noted as Caumil (meaning "No") in the vocabulary of words and phrases, as for instance "Caumil Murree" ("Not right"). This vocabulary was compiled nearly 50 years before the printing of the Rev. W. Ridley's book. But the difference of Kamil as we know it and Caumil as set down by Mrs. Dunlop is the difference noted in several instances between the same word pronounced by a tribesman from the interior and one from the coast. Concerning this an interesting philosophical comparison might be made with regard to "c" and "k" in the European languages. One illustration in Mr. Ridley's part of the district the tribes used "Kolle" as the word for water, and on the Wollombi the word was "Colly" or "Collie". I have also looked into Archdeacon Gunther's language of the Wiradhuri (Mudgee) and the language of the Wailwon on the Barwon, below the junction of the Namoi, where the Caumil or Kamil language was understood.

    Apparently there was what we in modern times call a "corridor" reaching from the coast about Gosford and running North West by the way of the Wollombi and the range, of which Burragurra form a part, to beyond the Liverpool Range, which in the Rev. Ridley's time was the home of the Kamilaroi [sic Gumilaroi] tribe. The route reached beyond there, for apparently the early explorers to the far north followed this ancient pad by which the Aboriginals made their treks or excursions. The tribe disappeared from the Wollombi very quickly in the 30's. We are told by Mr. W. A. Squire that a hundred years ago the Aboriginals could be counted by the hundreds, but in 1848 they numbered 54. Disease, of course had swept many of them away. Altered conditions of life killed others. But most of them followed the "corridor" into the interior. Whether the tribe came first from the coast and trekked inward; or came from beyond the Liverpool Range to the coast, is a matter for investigators of trade routes and tribal movements to look into. I will not venture at this juncture except to say there is evidence that the route stretches beyond the limits of the state of New South Wales into the extreme far north.

Names put on the map by the early surveyors of the Gosford District are of Comilaroi origin.

The interpretation of the rock carvings at Burragurra is therefore based on the vocabularies which I have been able to get together, but chiefly on the Comilaroi. From these I have taken directions like an explorer in a new country. The language tells the story.

These picture writings have been awaiting elucidation for many years, as did the Egyptian hieroglyphs as called by the ancient writers "The Words of the Gods." Here they are called "The Language that has brought the Light of God to the North." It was not until early in the 19th century that Thomas Young succeeded in deciphering the Egyptian Hieroglyphs. He was followed by the Champollion whose work gave the true base for our knowledge of Egyptian.

The word Hieroglyph means "sacred writing" and "Murree Gwalda" means practically the same. It will be noted as the story unfolds that writers ancient and modern have been the echoers of knowledge that had anticipated them by tens of thousands of years.

R. H. Matthews, the most prolific writer of ethnographical notes on the Aboriginals of Australia says in "Rock Carvings and Paintings of Australian Aboriginals" (1897), "most of the figures of animals were probably intended to represent the totems of different families, but it seems reasonable to suppose that some of the smaller drawings and nondescript devices are the result of idle caprice. The production of some of the larger groups – both of carvings and paintings has been a work of immense labour, and it is most unlikely that the natives would have taken so much trouble for mere amusement."

W. A. Squire, author of "Ritual, Myth and Customs of the Australian Aborigines," to whom Mr. W. J. Enright gave much information and was associated in the discovery of rock carvings in the Wollombi caves, says "There can be no doubt some definite purpose brought them into existence as man whose most trivial dances and actions had a fixed and important meaning would evidently do nothing but what would serve a practical purpose, and purely decorative art would, under the circumstances be scarce. But whatever their meaning was the Aborigines of today have either forgotten or never knew. All the figures are the outcome of untutored taste, the awakening art unconscious of the savage trying to express itself for some vague purpose." I quote Mr. Squire in preference to any other writer. He lived on the spot and had seen many of the carvings in the area. Where authorities are needed for other points of interest the names are given.

The discovery of these sculptures – the work of authors of the Stone Age – gives us first hand knowledge of the Aboriginals as recorded by themselves and a better interpretation of their ceremonies. The initiation into manhood ceremony is quite familiar. Many writers have made a study of what they call the "Bora," a word that has been carried from one end of Australia to the other by the Karaji, to express something which belongs to them. But few know anything about the meaning of the higher ceremonies, the interpretation which is given in this book.

Many have investigated the Karia, Guiyengaia (or as it has been written Gowargay and more recently by Professor Radcliffe Brown: Gayrage), Mirriwulla, Turramullan, (sometimes in the Wollombi referred to as Wa-booee), Mundowa, and Muun or Bahiame.

So much mysticism has been woven round these figures that the actual meaning of the words have been obscured. When the mystery is taken away from them and the myths that have grown up round them are removed one clearly sees a ritual in which is embodied and ethical system and what is more a history of the world.

More than a century has elapsed since these ceremonial grounds were used. The early residents of Wollombi who took an interest in the Aboriginals do not mention them, though possibly they were guarded from intrusion. In the hymns which were sung at these ceremonials which have also been preserved in the native language by Mrs. Dunlop, reference is made to two mountains Bolera-ngawl and Butherawuulay which were the names of two mountains on the Namoi. These mountains had some connection with Burragurra and Yango. Though they may have been on the maps under those names they may be identified by the description they give of themselves "Bolera-ngwal" means "A mountain with two heads" and "Butherawuulay" a "mountain that thrusts a sharp pointed top into the sky."

In view of the discoveries at Burragurra and Yango there might be found other ancient ceremonial grounds which still yield more knowledge.

The Namoi area was a centre of Aboriginal Lore and ancient ritual. The people in their language brought into common use many of the words used to denote symbols carved on the rock. This may indicate a heresy movement actuated by higher mental attainments believing that truth has nothing to conceal. Investigation shows that the cause of the numerous dialects is to be found in the difference of opinion on religious matters. Those who have broken away confusing their disputants by altering their language which has been received by the retort that "It is no language at all." These pictures and hieroglyphs were known to all who had been initiated no matter what dialect or language they spoke, or in what district they were found. The figures are also definitely distinguished by their features and attitude and by their number and their names which are written on every one of them.

Mrs. Dunlop's vocabulary is so full of information and meaning that it is possible that the only reason she did not leave behind the full story was due to the fact that she did not know of the existence of these ceremonial grounds. They had ceased to be used when the settlers got out that way. She mentions nothing about them. Her information was apparently gathered from the tribes who had an apparent trade route from the far interior to the coast by way of the Wollombi. Being a woman, that information was not given to her in full nor was the full purport of the words explained to her. For instance, she got hold of the sacred numbers just as numbers, but their real meaning is the key to the whole of the story from genesis to revelations. They are the key to the Egyptian theocracy and from them has evolved all religion, philosophy and science.

There were white men who had an intimate acquaintance with those Aborigines and from whom Mrs. Dunlop also gathered information. But even they had no acquaintance with the importance of numbers.

Among Mrs. Dunlop's manuscript notes are several songs which she did not attempt to translate. She was told they were difficult to put into the right meaning. These have remained until now undeciphered. They are in reality – apart from the initiation songs where the youth take on manhood – hymns of primordial man beautiful in conception and when put into the diction in which they thought them to be as beautiful as any hymns that have come to us from the remotest times. They explain the ceremonies which took place on the top of this [word cannot be recognised] mountains in the wilderness which has held its secret for so long. These hymns were not translated until I had written out the story from the words of the rock and confirmed my interpretation of the writing on the rocks.

Five of the songs belong to the first ceremony of the making of man, and six to the highest degrees to which they gradually advanced. In this book the higher degrees only are dealt with: The Creation, the Genesis of Man, the Resurrection and the Immortality of the Soul, together with other phases of the world's history.

Using the Murree Gwalda vocabulary as my guide and the picture graphs as the interpretation, I have been able to unravel the story of the rocks. I find however there is a system of writing in this huge book on the rocks – marking that we have been given the world its first lessons in setting down words.

In this respect the discovery has as much interest for the palaeographer as it has for the anthropologist and the archaeologist. It is the oldest form of writing in numbers, preceding the Egyptian Hieroglyphs from which all got their alphabets. The same system of numbering is found in the Hieroglyphic texts shorn of much of its glory, for the Egyptians made gods of the elements which the ancestors of Australian Aborigines only symbolised."[1]

Chapter 11

THE HOWS, WHYS, WHO AND WHERE

This is the last of the four introductory chapters that sets out the 'goal posts and playing field' and focuses on the lynchpin of Slater's research: Murree Gwalda[1], the first Language spoken throughout the planet. It is in this chapter Slater provides the refences and sources that underpin his interpretations.

He sets out a very fluid movement and interchange of tribes, "stretching beyond the limits of New South Wales into the extreme north."[2] That seems to run counter to how tribes were more secular and insular in culture and dealings when the British Invasion began, there is an assumption that each tribe had always kept very close to home-base. Dreaming stories were for the most part related to their tribal estates, and most resources and food was tied into where they lived. There is no talk or suggestions of tribes being directly connected with others thousands of kilometres to the north, or in any other direction.

Figure 46: Southern Law Confederation[3]

But Karno has told us many times of earlier days when we "had more DNA"[4] functioning and there were three confederations of tribes that spanned the entire continent. During these ancient times his tribe, the Ramindjeri, were part of the *Southern Law Confederation*[5]. Being one of three affiliations that covered all of mainland Australia, it spread across the continent encompassing the coastal land from Cape York (Qld) all the way around to Victoria and on to the Kimberleys (W.A.), and went inland "three hundred miles."[6] Within each confederation, sacred objects travelled freely, specific stones that suited blades, flakes and axes were traded, and so too ceremonies sometimes were about all over the country and welcomed guests. Although never specifically stated or delineated, we suspect the second confederation was a fair amount of inland Australia and the third the northern Top End. What was made clear was that within each of three confederations there was constant contact, trade, interaction and conversation.

Syntax and Semantics

Further on in his book Slater goes into considerable detail when discussing the technicalities of the Murree Gwalda language. He did provide a basic explanation in his letters to his Standing Stones assistant Fordham. He stated that there are ten principal words, all have four different meanings which are reliant on the accompanying text as to which meaning is implied. To that principle base load, another seven sensory words were added. From that somewhat deceptively meagre base of seventeen, he made note of the addition of twenty odd suffixes and even more prefixes that could be added. He also spoke about how these ten base works could be broken down or reconstituted, in fact, according to his analysis this ancient global language comprised of no less than twenty-eight-thousand words.

In compiling this ancient dictionary, he referred to the work of Reverend William Ridley[7] and R.H. Matthews[8] and rightly accords them a secondary status, but it is Eliza Hamilton Dunlop who put together what Slater referred to as the Great Record Book, who he cites as his primary source of knowledge. Slater acknowledged that "my chief source of assistance in investigation, however, has been an unpublished manuscript of the sacred language as spoken around the Wollombi by Mrs. David Dunlop."[9] Murree Gwalda not only means First Language it "really means "The Soul" or the "spirit" language or the language which brought the light of God to the earth."[10]

Figure 47: R.H. Matthews[11]

There are two immediate issues that just do not fit into our perspective of how humans evolved that needs to be fully appreciated. At a pragmatic level Slater wrote in one of his eighteen letters to Fordham that this language had a vocabulary of at least twenty-eight thousand words. Most humans use up to five-thousand words and quite a few far less.

The expectation was that as we go back in time our languages were progressively less in numbers and began at its most limited, crudest and basic in subject matter. What Slater has interpreted is the diametric opposite of what every text and curriculum insist as facts. Moreover, it is not just the expectation that the first words were so primitive and barely numbered in three figures in total that is under question, but when it comes to the content Slater interpreted, that is so beyond the realms of everywhere here.

If the first language ever spoken is indeed "The Words of the Gods,"[12] with its purpose being to bring the "Light of God,"[13] then just saying one word carries with it obligations. If you are speaking God's tongue, then surely every word uttered will be heard by these same Gods. It is a form of 'royal telephone,' but one from which you can never hang up. Knowing once speaking this language there are no secrets, but there will be consequences that 'fit the crime' if a mistake is made, is a great incentive to be fair and just in word and deed.

Such descriptions may seem a touch nebulous and decidedly lacking in any empirical foundation, but as long as one remembers one of Slater's guiding rules being the enrichment of the soul is the main topic of these ancient days, all the language was doing was reflecting the main esoteric concerns and aspirations we held when we had "more DNA." The best way to get a deeper appreciation for what this first global language addressed is to share a selection of translations Slater made when examining the markings on some of massive Standing Stones Complex near Mullumbimby (NSW), they give a snippet of something so precious and sadly forgotten during recent times.

Before directly quoting from Slater interpretations from the stone monoliths, to walk straight in without first giving the conventional understanding of how our first spoken language came about is essential if trying to understand why such a 'hatchet job' was about to come to trash everything with which Slater was associated. Very briefly and clearly incorrect, the experts assure us the first language spoken by ancient humans was supposedly crude in construction limited to the most basic concerns in content and sparse in quantity and nuances. Slater is adamant that this soul language is the absolute opposite in every respect.

"Enter and Learn the Truth of the Divine Light."[14]

"The Breath of God is the Divine Light of the Soul."[15]

"The light of Truth flows like a river of fire from God to the soul of man and woman united."[16]

"Guided by Truth man came to earth through darkness from the light of life that shines far off."[17]

"The soul of man came from the Immortal Light to drink the water of life from God."[18]

"Man (life) came to earth as man with his senses (seven of them) and was established in Truth."[19]

"God came in with Light from Darkness and gave man a soul and the sons of man brought in with light became the pillars of heaven."[20]

"He who brought life into the world, set down man and woman and gave them the sacred means of propagating life."[21]

Seriously, what ancient mainstream religion addressed humans as collectively being "man and woman?"[22] There is not skerrick of gender bias, we are utterly equal. Equally, the phrase "came to earth"[23] is used more than any other term in his interpretations of the Standing Stones site. And what is equally revealing is that in coming to earth it is always a passage through "darkness"[24] (space). The experts never suggested or even suspected that the First Language is riddled in metaphors. Nor did they propose the content repeatedly recorded the issues of divinity, the overriding importance of the soul and truth. And then to only reinforce the undeniable existence of the metaphysical, Slater talks about humans having the "sacred means of propagating life."[25] And in doing so humans had not just the five "senses"[26] with which we are now familiar, but two more that have been lost or stolen since the beginning. If Slater is actually right then it is true his hypothesis that Murree Gwalda is indeed a language that came from a time that was far more evolved and insightful, then everything that follows down the linear language timeline we have mistakenly constructed is no less than second-rate, and often much worse.

The "Corridor"[27]

This "corridor"[28] Slater mentioned but never fully understood the full extent of what he was hinting at, but did not extend. When explaining why the numbers of local Originals was drastically reduced, alarmingly so, he clearly acknowledged mischief, bullets and poison were horrific factors, but along with this deliberate genocide Slater did propose a 'get out of jail' card through a corridor that extended not only to Gumilaroi land, but further on and out of state to the far north of Queensland. He was quite confident that this trek extending thousands of kilometres was so, but if he went a little further in wondering why, with Original people all over suffering as did this tribe, that meant more of the same woeful times for all. It was terrible for all the tribes.

Under these extremely trying and fatal times, everything was stretched or in short supply, including food through reducing the time available to hunt and gather. Then all of a sudden there are at least a hundred extra mouths to feed and build extra shelters, that is a massive imposition when these newcomers know nothing of their ceremonies, even less about the Guardian spirits and they barely have enough to go around to begin with. Nonetheless, they were greeted and cared for is if they were their own. They had to, because as Karno said repeatedly that in ancient times Australia was divided into three Confederations of Tribes, and that secret business wasn't lost as the invasion began to take hold and was always the final word.

That being the Original truth, factoring the geography of the Southern Law Confederation that ran along the coast of Australia from Cape York to the Kimberleys and went three hundred miles inland, and throughout that tribal consensus everyone within looked after anyone from the collective if hard times fell upon them. In those first years of invasion and warfare. Old Ways prevailed and unity was essential throughout each confederation, and everyone stood together helping each other in every possible way.

Undeniably a Brilliant Record but Incomplete

Slater's first port-of-call in his research is obviously Dunlop's stunning research and record, but he openly concedes it is an excellent primary source that does have a few gaps and omissions. Understandably so, as Eliza Dunlop was a woman and the Wollombi Elder who was sharing everything he could was fully aware there is women's business, men's business and general business. Slater pointed out that her "acquaintance with the importance of numbers"[29] was limited to counting and went no deeper, as it should be.

What was even more of a hindrance was that it seemed that all or most ceremonies were no longer being conducted. Without ceremony the knowledge of sacred matters and the First Language will be and was severely depleted. Some of these male gaps were partially rectified through the work of the two men he referenced, but equally, some gaps and blanks still remain. As for trying to gain any knowledge of secret business and the intricacies of the first mother-tongue of Murree Gwalda from the few Original remaining, Slater had three hurdles to overcome in that for nearly all still surviving such things were forgotten, never known or there was a refusal to divulge secret business to White-fellas who had not been given the proper ceremonies first.

Nevertheless, what was left over was still sufficient in providing a general complexion and direction, and Slater was certainly walking down the right path and had only the best of intentions.

Onwards and Upwards

That concludes Slater's introduction and general themes he will now expand upon in so many ways, he has provided the framework of his research, from this point on it is time for the proof, content and esoteric insights and motivations understood during very ancient times to be presented and 'fleshed out.' Slater claimed this narrative dealt with issues like the "destiny of Man,"[30] "creation"[31] and "the words of the Gods"[32] which are part of this narrative on stone, and right now such knowledge is both so lacking and so needed.

Frederic Slater is a genuine, honest man, he was given the Great Record Book and had a choice, walk away or dive into the divinity and wisdom of the past and enjoy the ride. He chose the truth and all that it entails, both the good and bad. With the planet now rapidly ascending and its resonance amplifying, the same choice is now on offer to every soul on this planet. Hopefully, we have now cleared away some of the obstacles, mischievous fabrications and slanderous allegations so that when reading his precious gift and legacy from so long ago, the forgotten origins and wisdom of the past will become the future for those of us granted the right to remain.

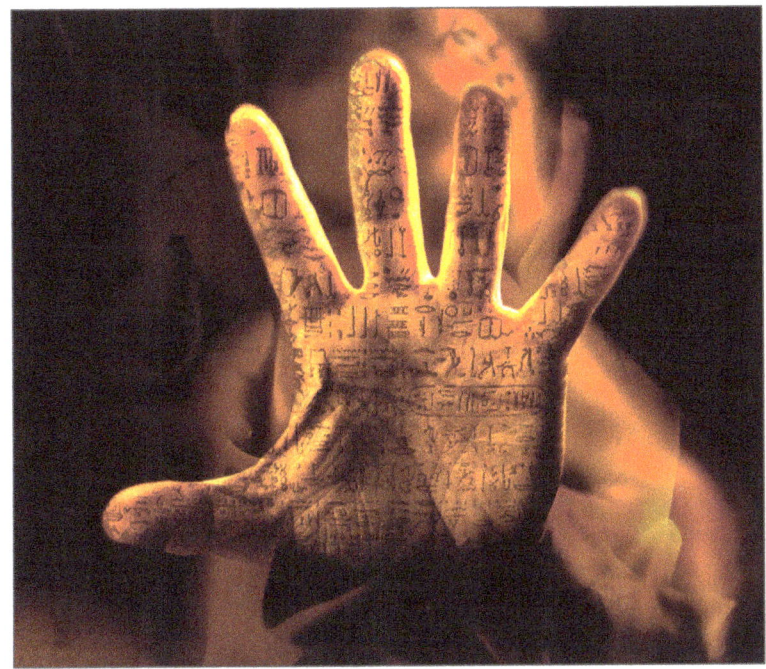

Figure 48: Great Record Book[33]

Chapter 12

FINDING NEMO

Finding Nemo is an animated child's movie that is focussed on a baby fish that has trouble learning or remembering. He relies on others for literally everything, so much so he cannot find his way home unless his parents mark out the direction to proceed. He tends to forget nearly everything he is shown and to begin with, is incapable of any independent thought or observation. One may ask why we even raised this fictional narrative, but the reality is it is so pertinent and merely a statement of cause and effect. The film is all about Nemo trying to find his way back home, and equally, finding his own voice and home-base.

Figure 49: Nemo[1]

The same issues are addressed by Slater. All of his work was for some time lost or hidden, but this is not about Slater as he was merely the messenger delivering truths that very few wanted to hear or receive. Above and beyond the picking and choosing, what is inconvenient is something more essential that was lost in translation and derision. We believe the central issue relates to what was brought to this planet in its embryonic form and was marginalised, ridiculed and then stolen. Slater tells us that man came to earth with "senses (seven of them)."[2] Well, if so, it seems two of these insights/talents are no longer functioning, as every scientist and medical expert will assure us that the number can only be five. It was only after these two esoteric talents were stolen or hidden, that we lost our foresight, and we are no longer a soul taking up temporary residence in a flesh and bone body, but merely someone who accepts the oft heard mantra of 'you only live once.' We have now chosen to live in a place where 'what you see is what you get.'

Slater believes that we have been in a constant spiralling descent since the beginning. He is adamant that when we began it was as good as it ever was. The beginning was a symbiotic harmonious interplay between spirit, soul and flesh and bone where we knew all about "Creation"[3] and the "Destiny of Man."[4] Way back then humans understood why we are here and why we come and go. That was then, now everything is so different and so desperately shallow.

Slater's research and interpretations are all about what was lost, stolen and sneered at. It is the two senses missing, that changes everything. What it does mean from a mathematical standpoint is that today humans are not running on 'six cylinders' as we are at least 28% below optimum efficiency. Back then Karno insists that we "had more genes,"[5] fast forward to today and the experts assure us about 90% of our genetic coding serves no purpose beyond spectating.

In the beginning everything made sense, as for today it is all about filling in the gaps. Slater states that he has the "key"[6] in the pages of his book, this is definite, but what is it this key can unlock? According to his interpretation of the First Language engraved into rocks the answer is so simple. This truth is engraved and repeated so often on the rocks, and it always comes down to the Soul first, and daylight second. As Slater would reply in his work the main reason, we incarnate on this planet is for our souls to be civilised.

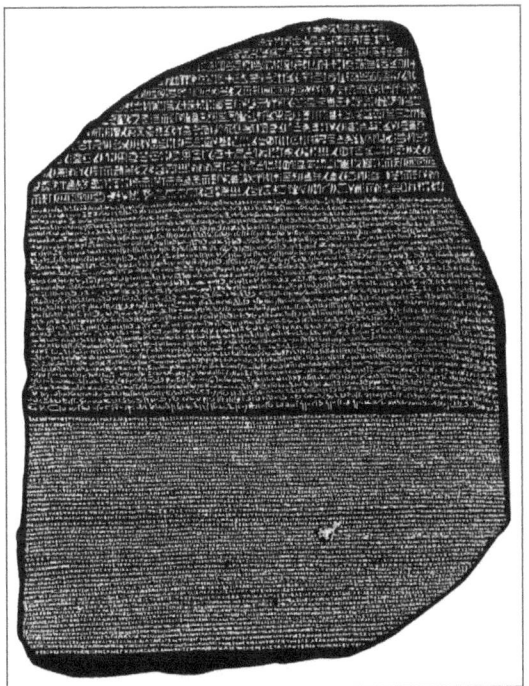

Figure 50: Rosetta Stone[7]

What needs to be acknowledged is that this book of Slater's has no equal. It is the secret history and philosophy of the Original people of Australia, that goes all the way back to the beginning and is somewhat like a printed version of the Rosetta Stone, but with the translation already supplied. However, unlike the Rosetta Stone[8], which is Egyptian hieroglyph specific, Slater's work has global implications as his translation relates to one language spoken throughout the world by everyone. Moreover, the script on the Rosetta Stone was a public record dealing with the mundane and profane, whereas Murree Gwalda was more mystical in persuasion and was all about the Soul Language and issues of the Spirit. There is no other book, ancient document or tablet on this planet that is its compatriot in importance or stature.

Figure 51: Blue Kachina Star Prophecy[9]

What remains after all the mystical collateral damage is a corrupt brew with a suspicious crew, and it hurts. If we were at our very best so long ago, then Slater's interpretations will guide us back to where it all began, but only if still seeking the Old Way answers. But it is not just Slater recommending that we re-connect with the Old Ways, the Hopi[10] have a prophecy called the Blue Kachinas[11], which speaks of a time of transformational change on the planet. They believe this time is now upon us and warn every soul that no-one is guaranteed a 'ticket to ride,' unless they understand and embrace the Old Teachings. Slater said the exact same things, but eighty years earlier.

With a solid base established by Slater in the first four chapters and his paper on Burragurra what comes next is the content and proof. It changes everything, and it is not just an historical account of what happened so long ago, but the blueprint of how things should be in the immediate future. We believe this Earthly renaissance is nearly here, but as to who will be here to be part of this ascension, that is an individual choice with long-term consequences.

For any who still hold reservations or doubts over Slater's suitability or integrity, there is still one more piece of very empirical, very hard, extremely metallic and clearly unambiguous evidence testifying to Slater's character and "high esteem"[12] in which his colleagues regarded him.

Chapter 13

NOBODY CARED

Of recent days, with this massive influx of newspaper clippings about Slater, most of the critiques have lessened. However, even though the evidence validating his credentials through the extensive coverage he received that cannot be challenged, there still is one final 'loop-hole' the critics cling to. Now with their denial of any recognition or publicity garnered through the press dismissed, their revised rebuttal is coated in indifference. In the simplest terms he was a pest with a forum of very few and ignored or quietly sniggered at when 'push came to shove.' They quote from no printed source citing a contesting article, or even provide some anecdotal proof in support, it is just blanket denial of everything he did being of no interest or academic credence.

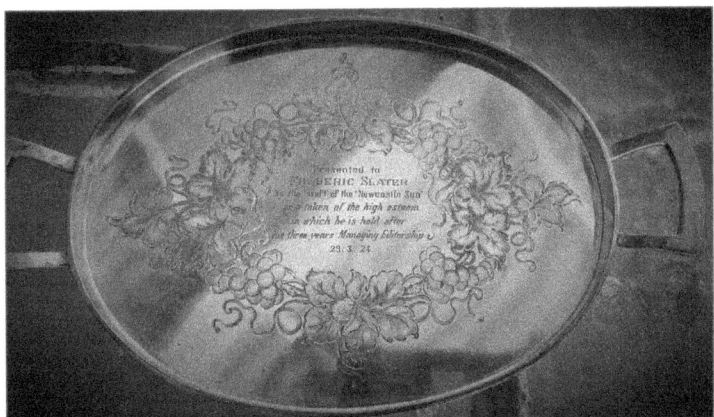

Figure 52: Frederic Slaters Award[1]

Undeniably the people speaking on behalf of his family agreed that nothing "at all"[2] was of value. But current events even call that denial into question, as some financial worth was gained once by someone in the family selling Slater's 1922 commemorative plate earning a sizeable profit running into three, or maybe even four, ten-dollar notes.

Even though the family readily stated that he was a charlatan and that nothing he did should be taken seriously, the people who worked for and with him clearly disagreed. After his fourth stint of "managing editorship,"[3] this time around at the *Newcastle Sun* from 1922 to 1924, during which the readership numbers doubled, he was given this parting gift by his colleagues. What was engraved on the silver platter speaks for itself and Slater as well.

"Presented to FREDERIC SLATER by the staff of the *"Newcastle Sun"* as a token of the high esteem in which he is held after his three years Managing Editorship. 29. 3. 24"[4]

Figure 53: Frederic Slater's Award (close-up)[5]

The upshot of this gift is a division, either his immediate family is wrong about everything they said about Slater, or his staff are mistaken, it has to be one or the other. In deciding which opinion is correct, it must be remembered that the many other reports on Slater are always complementary and never insulting. Apart from the delicate filigree patterns that surround this dedication to Slater, the words chosen make it clear that this man was very successful as a journalist, poet, fictional and non-fictional author.

Jon Wyatt found this personal award listed for sale by a Canberra Antique dealer. Knowing that many of Slater's relations of today live in Canberra, it seems quite logical to assume someone from the family sold this at this shop, and the selling price was $75, it would make sense to predict the take home amount would be somewhere between $30-$40. That amount appears to be a paltry amount for something so personal and precious, yet after recent denials, so inconvenient. Since the interview about Frederic Slater with his family took place in 2017, I think it is reasonable to suggest that some of his family knew about the plaque. Whether it was disposed of to hide his legacy and credibility, or simply due to financial hardship where every cent counts, can never be definitively resolved. So, it all comes down to family or staff, but before passing a final judgement it needs to be known that Slater's marriage failed, and our understanding was that the separation was acrimonious, and that could have an influence on those who never knew or saw him. Hearing about conflict, when only half the story is welcome, is a bad base from which to construct or pontificate.

This plate and the "high esteem"[6] directed towards Frederic Slater is an empirical proof and truth engraved into silver. In the first place no scientist or archaeologist should be judged on his or her social skills, family relationships or political affiliations. At an even baser level, which is certainly the case right now in relation to Slater, gossip, hearsay and rumours should be avoided at all costs. Deciding whether Slater is a genius or mischievous should be done only after reading all of his work. The prescribed reading starts with Scribes of the Stone Age, then going through all eighteen letters, following on with the one co-paper we have, another five sent to us and then complete this reading list with a thoughtful examination of the words and sentiment etched into silver. Put that all together then top it off with a solid serve of hard evidence through "high esteem,"[7] and this, in combination, prepares the reader for the next section of Slater's interpretation which he calls the *Book of Translations*.

Figure 54: Book of Translations - More to Follow[8]

Chapter 14

GODDARD'S REPORT BY ROY GODDARD

"Devil's Rock, or Burragurra, is an isolated flat sandstone cap of the Hawkesbury sandstone, overlooking the Howe Valley which is more than 1,200 ft below. The nearest settlement is Dean's farm at Mogo Creek – 8 miles to the southeast. Few people ever visit this spot unless it is to hunt up staying cattle. Even then the approach would be via the Blaxland lines, an almost forgotten road from St. Albans – following the ridges to Fordwich. The Aboriginals probably made use of the track to go to and from the ceremonial ground at Burragurra, long before John Blaxland formed Fordwich Station on March 8, 1831.

Accompanied by Matthew Deans as guide, our approach was from Mogo Creek, a rough climb of about 1,000 ft for 4 miles to the west, until we met Blaxland's line. Following this in a northerly direction we kept to the main ridges. At about six miles from Mogo Creek, two large emu pads were observed as if travelling north. The measurements are 6 in. across the pad and 8 in. to the centre spur. These pads are about 31 ft. apart, and the carving in the rock surface 1 in. deep. Six inches to the north is a raised circular knob 12 in. in diameter. The knob is surrounded by a vein iron forming the lip of a quartzite rock. *Considerable weathering of the surrounding rock has elevated this knob about 3 inches.*

About a mile further up this ridge the track passes in a northerly direction across another sandstone outcrop, sloping away to the southwest. In the centre we observed two natural potholes 8 ft. apart and almost circular that on the western extremity measuring 18 in. diameter and 4 ft. deep. On the lower edge were several grooves made by the Aborigines. Two troughs have been made in the upper side, forming a catchment for this pothole. They measure 12 ft. and 14 ft. respectively. The pothole to the east measured 2 ft. in diameter and is 12 in. deep. On further examination of this area, the letters J. B. were discovered carved in the rock and evidently of considerable age. It was conjectured that as this track had been used by Blaxland in the early part of lasty century, that it is quite possible that the initials referred to John Blaxland of Fordwich. This natural catchment area has been improved by deepening with metal tools. This was the only water we found during the day and would in all probability be preserved by those early pioneers to refresh both man and beast on their travels to and fro.

At approximately 8 miles from Mogo Creek at the end of a spur of the range, branching away to the west of the track, there appears an isolated flat sandstone rock about an acre in extent towering above the surrounding country. This is the "Devil's Rock" or "Burragurra." About 5 miles to the west is Yango Mountain rising 3,345 feet above sea level, and beyond, a few points to the southwest, The Chimney Stack or Tyan Peak at Capertee can be discerned. Mount Werong is to the north, and beyond is Mount Murwin or Howe's Mount.

There are some remarkable carvings depicted on Devil's Rock. They were not easy to discern at first owing to the heavy snow clouds hanging about. Fortunately, there was a break in the clouds for a short period, and with the lengthening rays of the sun the carvings showed up in sharp relief, long enough to make our records.

These carvings include several figures of men and animals, birds, tracks and circles.

Approaching from the east we observed 10 emu pads each 3 ft apart, and leading to the first carving, which has so weathered that the complete outline of the figure- apart from the trunk and snout- could not be traced. Two feet to the northwest is a carving 4 ft in length resembling a dog. Four feet west is the first of three spirit pads carved 1 in deep 12 in. long by 8 in. wide, travelling in a northerly direction. These pads are also 3 ft. apart. The third pad forms part of another carving of a woman's figure measuring 5 ft. to extremities. Three feet to the west is the most striking figure carved on Devil's Rock, depicted in what is apparently a sitting posture, with one arm outstretched to the north.

It appears to have five eyes. It measures 4 ft. in length from the extremity of the foot to the up-stretched hand and 2 ft. 3 in. across.

Heading away from the hand, towards the west, are four more emu pads 3 ft. apart to another remarkable figure 3 ft. 6 in. across with a craved snout. This figure appears to have three ears or an emu pad at the apex and it is in a squatting attitude. The emu pads continue on beyond this figure across the whole face of the rock. The last emu pad is discerned on an isolated rock in the scrub. These emu pads are also about 3 ft. apart and are in a line with Yango Mountain.

At the third emu pad, from this last-mentioned figure, there is another emu track branching off at right angles and leading due north again. Eight emu pads were observed in this direction and are also placed 3 ft. apart.

From the up stretched hand of the leading figure there is another track leading to the southwest, forming three emu pads 3 ft. apart, to the figure of a man measuring 4 ft. in length with 5 rays spreading from his hand and with arms outstretched as in the former figure. Three feet to the west is another figure 2 ft. in length of trunk, arms outstretched and fore shortened legs. Heading away to the south 7 more emu pads were observed also 3 ft. apart. The most prominent rise in the region in the ranges in this direction is Mount Wilson, with Mount Irvine just below its ridge.

Four feet to the west is a bird-like figure with what appears to be a bird's leg coming from the breast. Eight feet from this figure are two carved circles 12 ft. apart and 22 in. in diameter. Three feet to the south is another emu pad 5 in. in length leading to another remarkable figure 2 ft. in width, but owing to the disintegration of the rock it is hard to discern the full outline. Twelve inches further south is a short animal which is probably representing a wombat. Six feet beyond are two more circles 10 in. and 15 in. in diameter respectively. A small snake 12 in long is also depicted nearby. There are many other tracings of carvings, but owing to the disintegration of the rock surface they could not be properly discerned, and like most Aboriginal rock carvings they are lost for all time.

On January 25, 1936, we investigated the area at Yango Mountain but found it consisted of a volcanic cup the stone being of too hard a nature to be worked by primitive tools. Descending we made for a ridge separating the head waters of Yango Creek and a branch of the Macdonald River. Here we came across a natural clearing of level headland at the end of the sandstone ledge. This appeared to be an old camping ground where the Aboriginals mustered for their ceremonies. The first carvings we came across were two emus 3 ft. from head to tail and 1 ft. 8 in. across the back. Fifty feet to the southeast is a figure similar to the figure at Burragurra, with rays spreading from the head; but in this figure there are eight rays instead of five. There are two boomerangs, one above the right hand and the other at the left foot. The figure also has five eyes and a girdle at the waist. The length of the figure is eight feet. Twenty feet due south is a similar figure 5 ft. long and 1 ft. in width holding a boomerang in the right hand and without rays spreading from the hand. Attached to it is a similar figure. Continuing in a semi-circle for 4 ft. is another of these figures 6 ft. in length by 4 ft. in width lying across a coolamon or shield. The other figures complete the semi-circle. The intervening spaces of the circle to the first figure has weathered and any drawings that may have been there have almost disappeared."[1]

Appendix 1

"DISCOVERY OF AUSTRALIA BY DE QUIROS IN THE YEAR 1606" BY PATRICK F. CARDINAL MORAN, ARCHBISHOP OF SYDNEY.

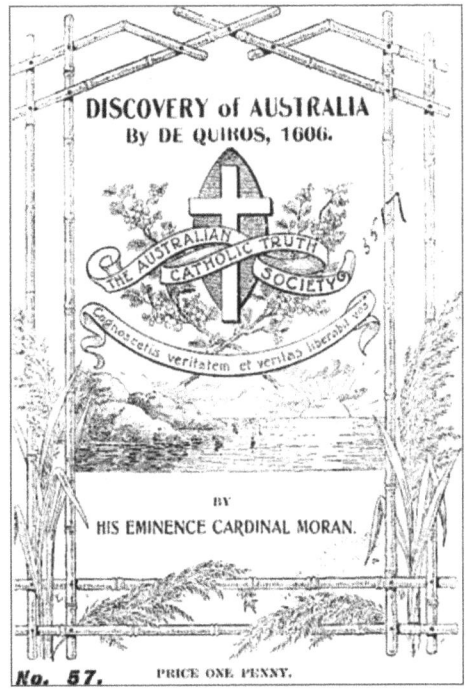

Pedro Fernandez de Quiros was the least of the brilliant galaxy of Portuguese and Spanish explorers who throughout two centuries, by their maritime skill and enterprise, won immortal fame for their respective countries, and extended far, to the east and to the west the limits of Christian civilisation. He was a Portuguese by birth, but at the period of which we treat Portugal and Spain were united under the Spanish sceptre, and hence it was under the Spanish flag and by the aid of the Spanish court that he achieved his discoveries.

The most famous or his expeditions was that which led to the discovery of the Great Austral Land in 1606. The original sources, however, which would serve to illustrate this expedition were little better than a sealed book to English readers, till Mr. W. A. Duncan, Fellow of St. John's College, published in Sydney, in 1874, the Spanish text and translation of an interesting Memorial, addressed by De Quiros to the Spanish monarch. A few years later Don Zaragosa, a distinguished Spanish ecclesiastic, published at Madrid in three volumes the same Memorial, together with several other invaluable con-temporary documents illustrative of De Quiros's voyage. The learned president of the Hakluyt Society, Sir Clements Markham, has published in two volumes in London, for the Hakluyt Society, in 1904, a translation of these important records, with a valuable introduction and several interesting notes.

Till within the last few years the opinion very generally prevailed that the Island of Santo, the chief island of the New Hebrides, was the Great Land discovered by De Quiros. In the History of the Catholic Church in Australia I ventured to dissent from that opinion, and since then several papers bearing on the subject have appeared in the public press and in the Proceedings of the Geographical Society of Melbourne.

{Page 2}

I propose in the present discourse to submit the claims of Australia to be the Great Southern Land thus discovered it 1606 by De Quiros, and the better to proceed with order in the inquiry, my remarks will be comprised under the following heads:--

I. I will present to you from the original narratives some extracts descriptive of the Great Southern Land which was discovered by the Spanish explorer.

II. It will readily be seen that the data furnished by these extracts are inconsistent with the claim of the Island of Santo to be that newly-discovered land.

III. On the other hand these data are found to accurately fit in with the claim of Port Curtis and the adjoining Queens-land coast.

IV. Some arguments shall be considered that seem to favour the Island of Santo's claim.

V. The difficulties will be solved that are advanced against the Australian claim.

VI. We will thus be free to conclude by presenting some interesting details of the expedition of De Quiros and of the festivities with which he and his companions inaugurated the discovery of this Australian Continent.

I.

1. I will take my first extracts from the 8th Memorial presented by De Quiros to the Spanish King in 1607, published by Sir Clements Markham. De Quiros thus writes (IL, 478):--

"The greatness of the land newly discovered, judging from what I saw, and from what the captain, Don Luiz Vaez de Torres, the Admiral under my command, reported to your Majesty, is well established. Its length is as much as all Europe and Asia Minor as far as the Caspian and Persia, with all the islands of the Mediterranean and the ocean which en-compasses, including the two islands of England and Ireland. That hidden part is' one-fourth of the world, and of such capacity that double the kingdoms and provinces of which your Majesty is at present the Lord could fit into it, and this without any neighbourhood of Turks or Moors, or others of the nations which are prone to cause disquiet and unrest on their borders."

He represents the discovered lands to be "antipodal to the greater part of Africa, to all Europe, and to greater Asia. The houses are of wood, roofed with palm leaves. They use pots

{Page 3}

of clay, weave cloths, and have clothing and mats of reed. They work Stone marble, and make flutes, drums, and spoons of varnished wood." (Sir Clements Markham has stone and marble, but there is no "and" in the original text, p. 480.) "The bread they have is made from three kinds of roots, of which there is great abundance, and they grow without labour, receiving no more help than being dug up and cooked. These roots are pleasant to the taste, very nourishing, and keep for a long time. They are a yard long and half a yard thick. The fruits are numerous and good. There are bananas of six kinds, a great number of almonds of four kinds, great obos, which are of the size and taste of peaches, many earth-nuts, oranges and lemons, which the natives do not eat, and another great fruit; and others not less good that were seen and eaten, as well as many and very large sweet canes. The riches are silver and pearls which I myself saw, and gold which was seen by the other Captain, as he says in his report...They have goats, and there were indications of cows...I declare that all that was seen and has been described is on the sea shore; so that it may be hoped that in the heart of the country such and so great riches will be found as are foreshadowed by what has already been seen. It is to be observed that my chief object was only to seek for the great land that 1 found... The comfort and pleasant life in such a land might be increased by the cultivation of its black, rich soil, by the erection of brick houses, by proper clothing, by working the marble quarries from which sumptuous and elegant edifices could be raised, and a land in which there is an abundance of timber for all sorts of work; where there are sites of plains, valleys and ridges, undulations, high mountains and thickets; and in which there are murmuring streams and springs; where might be erected any number of wind-mills, water-mills, sugar-mills, and other water engines; salt pits and sugar plantations. The sugar-canes, which grow to five or six palms and under, and the fruit in proportion, are witnesses of the richness of the soil. A slender, hard and smooth stone makes as good flints as can be, had in Madrid. The Bay of SS. Philip and James contains 20 leagues (60 miles) of shore, and is quite limpid, and is free to enter by day or night; it is surrounded by a large population; at a very great distance is seen by day much smoke, and at night many fires. The port of Vera Cruz (Holy Cross) is so

{Page 4}

capacious that it would contain at anchor 1000 ships. Us bottom is clear, and consists of dark sand. The worm that is so destructive to ships was not seen. Ships may be anchored at any depth from 4 to 4 fathoms, midway between two rivers, one of them (the Jordan) as large as the Guadalquivir, in Seville, with a bar of more than two fathoms, which frigates and patamars may cross. Our barques entered the other river freely, and took in fresh water, which is delicious in whatever part, out of the numerous streams there are, The landing place extends for three leagues and more on a strand of black pebbles, small and heavy, which would be very good for ships' ballast. The coast contains neither ruins nor rocks; the herbs on its banks are green; you hear not the sound of the tide; and as the trees are straight and not torn, I conclude there are no great tempests in that land. Moreover, this port, besides being so airy and pleasant,%has another great excellence for recreation, that. from the break of dawn you hear a very great army of warbling birds, some having the appearance of nightingales, larks, goldfinches,'and an infinity of swallows, parroquets, and a coloured parrot that was seen, besides a great many other birds of different kinds, and the shrill note of the locusts and grasshoppers. At morning and evening the sweetest smells are enjoyed from many kinds of flowers, among which are the orange and lemon blossoms; and I consider that all these and other effects are due to the excellence and regularity of the climate. At this port and bay are many excellent islands, several of which may be especially mentioned which subtend 200 leagues. One of them, about 12 leagues distant, is 50 leagues in circumference, and is very fertile and populous. And in conclusion, Sire, I say that in that bay and port a large and populous city may be built, and the people who will inhabit it may readily enjoy all riches and conveniences which, my small ability does not enable me to set forth. I do not exaggerate if I say that it can maintain and accommodate 200,000 Spaniards."

He further adds: "The temperature and salubrity of the air is seen in all that has been said, and in this, that we all being strangers, none fell ill during a time of working, sweating, and being wet through, without care about drinking water while fasting, nor about eating whatever the land produced, nor by the dew or sun or moon. The sun was not very hot

{Page 5}

by day, and from midnight onwards woollen clothes were sought, and very well suffered to be worn. The natives as a rule are strong and stout. Some are very old."

2. In a further Memorial presented to the King in 1601, he styles the land he had discovered a great land, "its double range of mountains and the River Jordan from its size appear to furnish evidence of the great. extent of the land." Besides Europe, Asia and Africa, there are only two great portions of the earth: "The first is America, which Christoval Colon discovered; the second and last of the world is that which I have seen, and solicit to people, and completely to discover for your Majesty."

He wishes it to be added to the royal realms "with the grand title of Australia del Espiritu Santo."

He ends: "If his suspicions led Christopher Columbus to complain, for me, what I saw, what I felt, and what I offer, makes me importunate."

3. One of the most interesting documents published by Zaragosa and Markham is a history of the Voyages of De Quiros compiled from his diaries by his secretary, Belmonte Bermudez, but signed and authenticated by De Quiros himself. From this narrative I glean the following extracts:--

On the 3rd of May, 1606, "the three vessels anchored in the port with great joy, giving many thanks to God...The Master of the Camp was sent to examine the mouth of the river, which is in the middle of the bay, with the launch, a boat and a party of men. He tried the depth of the river mouth, and found that there was no bottom, with the length of an oar and his own arm. He went further up in the boat, and the view of the river gave much pleasure to those who were with him, as well for its size and the clearness of the water as for its gentle current and the beauty of the trees on its banks."

They landed and found a small village; "they also found a flute, and certain small things worked out of pieces of marble and jasper...The bay has a circuit of 20 leagues, at the entrance four leagues across...In tie middle there is a river, which was judged to be the size of the Guadalquivir at Seville. At its mouth the depth is two and more fathoms; so that boats and even frigates could enter. It received the name of the Jordan. On its right is seen the Southern Cross

{Page 6}

in the heavens, which makes the spot noteworthy. To the eastward, at the corner of the bay, there is another moderate-sized river called Salvador, into which the boats entered at their pleasure to get water. The waters of both rivers are sweet, pleasant and fresh. The one is distant from the other a league and a half, consisting of a beach of black gravel, with small heavy stones, excellent for ballast for a ship. Between the two rivers is the port. The bread they use is mainly of roots...The rind is grey, the Pulp murrey colour, yellow, or reddish; some much larger than others (yarns). There are some a yard and a half in thickness, also two kinds; one almost round, and the size of two fists, more or less. Their taste resembles the potatoes of Peru. The inside of the other is white, its form and size that of a cob of maize when stripped.

Our people ate a great deal; and being of a pleasant taste and satisfying, they left off the ship's biscuit for them. These roots last so long without getting bad, that on reaching Acapulco those that were left were quite good. We heard, when on board at early dawn, a sweet harmony from thousands of different birds, apparently buntings, blackbirds, nightingales, and others. The mornings and afternoons were enjoy-able from the pleasant odours emitted from trees and many kinds of flowers, together with the sweet basil. A bee was also seen, and harvest flies were heard buzzing.

"The climate appeared to be very healthy, both from the vigour and size of the natives, as because none of our men be-came ill all the time we were there, nor felt any discomfort, nor tired from work...I am, able to say with good reason that a land more delightful, healthy and fertile; a site better supplied with quarries, timber, clay for tiles, bricks for founding a great city-on the sea, with a port and a good river on a plain, with level lands near the hills, ridges, and ravines; nor better adapted to raise plants and all that Europe and the Indies produce, could not be found. No port could be found more agreeable, nor better supplied with all necessaries, with-out any drawbacks, nor with such advantages for dockyards in which to build ships, nor forests more abundant in suitable timber good for futtock timbers, houses, compass timbers, beams, planks, and yards, Nor is there any other land that could sustain so many strangers so pleasantly, if what has been written is well considered. Nor does any other land have what this

}Page 7{

land has close by, at hand, and in sight of its port; for quite near there are seven islands, with coasts extending for 200 leagues, apparently with the same advantages, and which have so many, and such good signs, that they may be sought for and found without shoals or other obstacles, while nearly half-way there are other known islands, with inhabitants and ports where anchorages may be found. I have never seen, anywhere where I have been, nor have heard of such adavantages...

If we look round the coast of Spain, so good a port will not be found...It is to be noted that a cross, which had been left on the banks of the river Salvador, was found raised in its place, and that the natives had put branches and flowers round it."

He further writes that having come out from the port for departure "owing to the force of the wind, the ship, having little sail on, and her head E.X.E., lost ground to such an extent that we found ourselves 20 leagues to leeward of the port, all looking at those high mountains with sorrow at not being able to get near them."

On their return to the port of Acapulco (in Mexico), the cross of orange wood was presented to the Church of the Franciscans. It was on the 8th of December; feast of the Int. Conception, that the captain, "with the greatest solemnity possible, took the cross from the ship to the sea shore and delivered it to the Father Guardian." It was fastened to the high altar, and to mark the occasion there was "ringing of bells, sound of trumpets, and discharge of guns and arquebuses and muskets by the soldiers. All the people showed their joy; and not less did the captain, although he desired to go to Rome and put this cross in the hands of the Pontiff, and tell him that it was the first that had been raised in those new lands in the name of the Catholic Church."

4. De Torres, who was second in command of the expedition of De Quiros, addressed a letter to the King in 1607, giving some account of the voyage and of its various incidents.

Of the Bay he writes: "This Bay is very refreshing, and in it fall many and large rivers. In circuit it is 25 leagues. We named it the Bay de San Felipe y Santiago, and the land that of Espiritu Santo...At length we sailed from this bay, in conformity to the order, although with intention, to sail, round this island; but the season and the strong currents would

{Page 8}

not allow this, although I ran, along a great part of it. In what I saw. there are very large mountains. It has many ports, though some of them are small., All of it is well watered with rivers. We had at this time nothing but bread and water: it was the height of winter, with sea, wind, and ill-will (of the crew) against us. All this did not prevent me reaching the mentioned latitude (30 deg. S.), which I passed one degree, and would have gone further if the weather had permitted; for the ship was good…Going into the said latitude on a. S.W. course, we had no signs of land that way. From thence I stood back to the N.W. to 11 1/2 S. Latitude; there we fell in with the beginning of N. Guinea. I could not weather the E. point, so I coasted along to the westward on the S. side."

5. We have also the diary of Gaspar de Leza, who was Chief Pilot of the expedition, and whose shrewd incidental remarks are particularly interesting. He writes that the Bay "received the names of St. Philip and St. James, the 1st of May, the day of discovery, being the day of those apostles. The bay is very large and beautiful, and all the fleets of the world might enter it."

2nd May. The General said: "that there were signs of great things in that bay; for although we had been two days within it, we had not yet seen the end of it, because it was so large."

4th May. "At two in the afternoon our General went, with the two boats and an armed party, to see the river. Coasting along it was seen that there were many streams flowing from a beautiful plain, on which cities might be built, for it must have been ten leagues in extent. In another part there were many hills, high and low, with beautiful plains. In most of those hills, except the main range, one might ride on horse-back over them.

5th May. "Our boat went further along the coast and discovered another river, which flows very grandly over the plain, so that frigates could go up to it. This river flows into the middle of the bay, about a league from the other where we were anchored, and there were several streams."

8th May. "Our tender went to examine the coast, and reported that they had coasted along and had seen beautiful plains and rivers that fell into the sea, and that all was well peopled by natives, who came out on the beach to see them.

{Page 9}

They seemed to, cover the land, for up to the mountain tops all was inhabited. The land is so fertile that it yields plenty of food, and it is so fresh that it obliges a man to cover him-self with a blanket, a state of things to which we were not at all accustomed."

10th May. "We returned to the shore, and, marching in-land, came to their houses, finding them abandoned. From the sea, by the inland forest, the distance is about half a league. Round the houses were many fruit trees, with inter-twined palisades, by reason of the great quantity of pigs. All was very well arranged, the houses and yards being very clean. We found many fruits and trees of different sorts...The road is very clean and well shaded, and there are beautiful streams of water. From midnight until morning there is a pleasant coolness, which makes a blanket welcome."

11th May. "We found ballast as good as that of Callao, and just like it, consisting of small pebbles."

14th May. Feasts of Pentecost. He gives the names of the municipality and officers appointed for the new city to be founded.

17th May. "We climbed up a high mountain very silently, and from the top we discovered a beautiful plain. On descending to it we found much nutmeg and almonds of a different kind, for the rind smells like an apple, and another fruit with smell and taste like a nectarine. Of all these fruits the woods were full, and there is scarcely a tree in all this land that is not of some use, so that here one might live in great luxury."

19th May. "This day in the morning, and the day before at" night, there were great tremblings of the earth, some of them lasting an hour, and we felt them on board our ships, as if they were bumping on some rock. From this we concluded that where there are such great earthquakes it must be the mainland, as it also seemed from the mountain ranges. As soon as we came on board, our General wanted a party to go and fish at the great river, to which the name of Jordan was given. The river whence we got the water was named Salvador."

20th May. We went to the river Jordan, which is two leagues from the port where the ships were at anchor...Our people found great quantities of fruit trees, and much food with which these natives are well supplied. Great quantities

{Page 10}

of fish were caught. Ships might enter this river, if they were built like the frigates of Carthagena."

28th May. "We started in the morning, coasting along the land to windward, that is, to S.E. and E.S.E., to make out for certain whether it was the mainland

29th May. "On account of many of the crews being sick (from eating poisoned fish) they returned to the bay. This was at 7 o'clock in the morning, and by 4 o'clock in the after-noon the ships had anchored. This was good luck, for the distance from the entrance to the bay to the anchorage is six or seven leagues, and the first time we were three days working up the

June 5th. "We were ready to start next day to examine 200 or 300 leagues of coast, surveying all, laying down positions of ports and anchorages, with soundings, rocks and banks, and latitudes."

6. Torquemada, who was Provincial of the Franciscans in Mexico, and derived his information from De Quiros and the chaplains of the expedition, published in 1614 a lengthened account of the celebrated voyage. He attests that the boats brought the report of "a very wide hay, sheltered from all winds...The captain and pilot, having heard the report on this bay, and of another great bay to leeward, ordered sail to be set; and so they proceeded, with no small joy.\ Ail had now been accomplished according to their desires, holding in their hands the most abundant and powerful land ever discovered by Spaniards...Presently the boat went to seek a convenient port, and brought news that there was one with soundings from four to six fathoms, all sand and clean, between the mouths of two rivers...As it was late they waited for another day, the 3rd of May, when they anchored, calling the port La Vera Cruz, and the land La Austral del Espiritu Santo."

"The port is between two rivers, and they gave one the name of Jordan, and the other the name of Salvador. Their banks are of no small beauty, for they are full of sweet flowers and herbs. The beaches of this bay are wide, long and flat.

In all parts facing the sea there are cool and pleasant groves extending to the sides of numerous hills, and even to the summit of one which was ascended by our people. These dills divide most fertile level valleys, which are picturesque,

{Page 11}

while the green bills are traversed by various rivers. The whole is a land which, without any doubt, has the advantage of America and of the greater part of our Europe." He further assigns the circuit of the Bay as 27 leagues, and the en-trance as having an expanse of eight leagues.

7. One of the most interesting records connected with tile ?e Quiros expedition is the manorial of Juan Luis Arias, a lawyer of Santiago in Chile, addressed to King Philip III. of Spain. He derived his information from the Franciscan Fathers who accompanied the expedition, and his memorial was written soon after the death of De Quires in 1615. He styles the newly discovered land "the Austral hemisphere," and he describes the harbour in which De Quiros landed as a magnificent expanse of water. "The land on the side that he first came upon ran from E. to W. It appeared to be more than 100 leagues (300 miles) long; the country was very populous, and although the people were dark, they were very well-favoured. There wore also many plantations of trees, and the temperature was so mild that they seemed to be in Paradise: the air also was so healthy that in a few days after they arrived all the men who were sick recovered. The land

produced most abundantly many kinds of very delicious fruits, as well as animals and birds in great variety. The bay was no less abundant in fish of excellent flavour and of all the kinds

which are found on the coast of the sea in Spain. The natives ate for bread certain roots like the batata (the yam), either roasted or boiled, which, when the Spaniards tasted, they found them better eating and more sustaining than biscuit."

He subsequently states that De Quiros reached the 26 deg. of S. Latitude, and adds: "The land of the Bay of San Felipe y Santiago showed very great signs of its being the coast of the southern continent; as much by its great extent as by there being visible from it, looming at a great distance, cordilleras of very lofty mountains, of very agreeable aspect; and by the fact of two rivers falling into the bay, one as large as the Guadalquivir, and the other not quite as broad; all signs of a continent, or at least of a very spacious and deep country approaching to a continent."

II.

The data which these extracts present cannot be reconciled with the Island of Santo's claims.

{Page 12}

1. The dimensions of Santo are given by Findlay in his "South Pacific Ocean Directory," published for the Admiralty in London in 1884. The Island of Santo, he tells us, is 65 miles in its greatest length, and about half that extent in its greatest width. Sir Clements Markham, in his Introduction, writes that Santo has a big bay, but is a small island. Some time ago one of our Sydney morning newspapers published a letter from a Protestant missionary, in which, he described his excursion across the island from shore to shore in one day.

Now it is quite absurd to suppose that expert explorers such as De Quiros and his companions were would be stationed at Santo for 36 days, and some of them for an additional term of 15 days, without their realising how limited was its extent. They describe the discovered land as of vast expanse, larger than Europe, even with Asia Minor and the Mediterranean added to it. One of its valleys that was spread out before them was 10 leagues (that is, 30 miles) in extent. They sailed along the coast for 100 leagues (300 miles), and felt assured, by its many rivers and well-sheltered ports, and by the splendid cordilleras that were seen in the distance, that they had alighted upon a vast continent. No rivers as are described in the ex-tracts can be found in Santo.

2. The Island of Santo is proud of its "big bay," but even this cannot be said to bear any proportion to the vast bay of SS. Philip and James, which was entered by De Quiros on 1st of May in 1606. The bay thus discovered was 20 leagues (60 miles) in length, and, according to De Torres, it was 25 leagues (75 miles) in circuit. One of the narratives gives it a circuit of 27 leagues, that would be 81 miles. The entrance to the Bay had an extent of eight leagues (24 miles), and at the entrance to the port it was four leagues (12 miles) broad. The pilot enthusiastically cries out that all the ships of the world would find room in that magnificent bay. How different are the proportions which Santo's bay presents! Findlay writes (p. 748) that the circuit of the bay of Santo is "about 36 miles." Sir Clements Markham (I. 273) inserts a report on the bay by Dr. Corney, a member of the Hakluyt Society, who visited it in 1876. He writes: "The depth or extent of the bay itself, from its chord formed by the imaginary E. and W. line drawn

{Page13}

through Cape Quiros, seemed to me about a dozen miles, and it is of similar width."

Mr. Panton, presiding at a meeting of the Geographical Society of Melbourne (Vol. xix., p. 80) in 1901, gave some. further details: "I have this day had the pleasure of meeting with the Rev. Mr. Paton, the well-known missionary of the New Hebrides, who, during 42 years' residence in that group, had often visited Santo. He informed me that the bay is 10 miles in depth, and about four or five miles across at the en-trance; that it is surrounded by wooded hills; that no distant sierra is to be seen from it; and that the one small river running into the Bay is named by the natives Yeor."

The bay discovered by De Quiros afforded safe anchorage, was "limpid and free to enter by day or by night," and was free from hurricanes. In Dr. Corney's description of Santo Bay (I. 274) we read: "The west shore of this bay rises steeply from the water throughout most of its extent...The anchorage, is not exposed either from E.N.E. or E.S.E., but from N.W. to N. and N.E. it is unsafe. Findlay writes of Santo Bay (p. 749): "The approach to Santo is not without its dangers...Hurricanes prevail during the whole of the wet season."

The discovered bay in its wide expanse faced the East, extending from N. to S. On the contrary, Santo Bay faces the north, extending from W. to E.

3. De Quiros particularly refers to the two rivers which flow into the bay, adjoining the port, the one as large as the Guadalquivir at Seville, the other not so large; both navigable, not to boats only, but to light frigates. Now at Santo there are several streams, but only one river. In the passage already cited by Mr. Panton, the Protestant missionary attests that there is but "one small river running into the bay." A Scotch planter of the New Hebrides, who was shipwrecked at Santo, and was compelled to spend several weeks on the island, writes: "Nowhere in Santo are there any such, rivers as are described by De Quiros in his account of the Tierra Australis; the tendency of all the streams on this island is to spread into shallows near the beach; that was my experience of them, and I have waded through them by day, and slept on their banks by night." ("Australasian Catholic Record," January, 1902.)

{Page 14}

4. What caused joy in a special manner to the Spanish explorers was that within the bay they found a splendid harbour, to which they gave the name of Vera Cruz, capable of safe anchorage for 1000 vessels. No such harbour is to be found at Santo Bay. Findlay curtly remarks: "The port of Vera Cruz is not to be found in it." Mr. Collingridge, in his most interesting "Discovery of Australia" (Sydney, 1895), also gives the statement of a venerable Marist missionary, who spent many years in the New Hebrides, that "there is no such port at Santo."

5. De Quiros and his associates refer to the fine strand connected with this port and extending

between the two rivers; and they make particular mention of the heavy black pebbles strewn on this strand, "admirably suited for ships' ballast." Nothing of all this is to be met with at Santo.

6. The narratives from which I have given extracts refer to the singular healthiness of the newly discovered land. Now Findlay writes of Santo (p. 749): "The climate from the luxuriance of the vegetation and the dampness of the soil seems much less adapted to European constitutions than the Polynesian islands, whose natives also suffer here from dysentery, fever and ague." The missionaries' reports confirm this statement. Mr. Bevan, addressing the Geographical Society of Melbourne in May, 1900, while eulogising the appearance of Santo, admitted the prevalence of "malaria and perpetual enervating heat," which made it unfit for Europeans.

7. No large islands are in sight from Santo Bay. De Quiros relates of the bay which he discovered that within view were seven islands, and midway to them other inhabitable islands. The circuit of the seven islands would be about 200 leagues, and one of them was 50 leagues (150 miles) in circumference, almost as large as the Island of Santo itself. The precision with which those Spanish explorers set forth the expanse of the islands off the discovered coast is a sure argument for their accuracy when they report the vast extent of the Great Southern Land.

8. De Quiros writes regarding the resources of the discovered land: "The riches are silver and pearls, which I saw, and gold which was seen by the other captain, as he says in his report." Findlay reports that in Santo there is nothing to indicate

{Page 15}

any such riches; "no trace has been found of silver or gold.

9. The various species of fishes which were found by the Spanish explorers are set forth in detail. Some of these, for instance the salmon and the pig-fish, are not to be found at Santo, but they have their habitat on the Australian coast.

10. Mention is made of the facilities for building which the marble quarries of the newly discovered land would pre-sent. No marble is to be found in Santo.

11. Findlay writes of Santo (p. 766): "It rather partakes of the character of an archipelago than a single island, from the numerous islands clustered around its shores." Such a prominent feature would not have escaped the careful inspection of De Quiros and his companions.

12. In describing the interesting features of the newly discovered land, the Spanish writers could not but have dwelt upon the attractiveness and beauty of its coral surroundings, were Santo the land to which they refer. Santo is justly classed among "the summer isles of Eden, in dark purple spheres of sea." Mr. Theodore F. Bevan, in his discourse al-ready referred to, at the meeting of the Geographical Society at Melbourne, in May, 1900, describes the vision that must have presented itself to the enraptured gaze of De Quiros when approaching

Santo: "Ocean floor bestrewn with emerald pearl and turquoise; rosy, like waking Venus, and after age-long sleep in blue Pacific depth the Great Cyclades uprose, homage to pay to their discoverer." All this could not have been for-gotten by De Quiros and his companions.

III.

The data furnished by the various memorials of De Quiros and his fellow-explorers fit in accurately with the claim of Port Curtis and the adjoining coast to be the Great Southern Land of their discovery.

1. To the newly discovered land they assigned the dimensions of a Continent. Such is Australia. We, must bear in mind that, believing it to be the long-sought-for Southern Continent, they would, in accordance with the current ideas in those days, extend its southern boundary to the Antarctic circle. With such limits, De Quiros might most justly estimate that it would exceed Europe even with Asia Minor and the Mediterranean

}Page 16{

superadded, and that it might justly be ranked a% a fourth part of the explored world.

2. The magnificent expanse of water, including Keppel Bay and Port Curtis, has an extent of about GO miles, and its circuit along the coast adds at least 15 miles to its length. The width of Keppel Bay at its entrance is about 24 miles, and that of Port Curtis is 12 miles. These measurements correspond in a general way with those that are assigned to De Quiros's discovery.

3. The Boyne and Calliope Rivers correspond to the two rivers described by De Quiros. Their position "midway in the bay," adjoining the anchorage, and the distance of about six miles between the mouths of the rivers, correspond to the description given in the extracts. De Torres writes that other rivers also fall into the bay, and here we have the Fitzroy and other smaller rivers. It might at first cause surprise that De Quiros would not make special reference to so important a river as the Fitzroy. But we must bear in mind he was in search of anchorage and of navigable rivers. The Boyne and Calliope were just the rivers that met his wishes. The Fitzroy, with its rocky approaches, repelled the Spanish navigators, and it was only when the rocks were cleared at considerable expense in latter times that it became at all navigable.

4. Port Curtis, or as it is at present more generally called, Port Gladstone, is precisely such as would captivate the heart of De Quiros. "A thousand ships could find anchorage here," is his description of the newly discovered port. It will be remarked as a singular coincidence that some years ago Mr. Nesbitt, examining the coast harbours on the part of the Government, officially reported in almost identical words: "The harbour of Port Curtis offers safe anchorage for 1000 of the largest vessels afloat."

In an official despatch of Colonel Barney to the Government under date 20th July, 1847, we read: "The position and extent of Port Curtis, which I take to be the third harbour in importance in these seas, inferior only to Port Jackson and Hobart Town, must shortly lead to an establishment on its shores."

5. A remarkable feature of the strand at Port Curtis is that it is strewn with "black heavy pebbles" such as De Quiros describes. These are the "Manganese bubbles," as they are

{Page 17}

locally designated. The editor of the "Gladstone Advocate," in a letter to me, writes: "Manganese abounds in this district. Fragments of this mineral, black and heavy; are strewn all over the shore line when the tide goes out." I may add that one of the richest mines of Manganese has its opening close to the present harbour landing place at Gladstone.

6. There is no question as to the healthiness of the Queensland coast, and to the invigorating influence of its atmosphere, particularly in the months of May and June, which was the time of De Quiros's sojourn there.

7. The seven islands within sight, and other inhabited islands half-way, are a distinctive feature of Keppel Bay and Port Curtis. One of the distant islands, with a circuit of 50 leagues (150 miles), corresponds to Curtis Island. Facing Island, in front of Gladstone, was inhabited by the natives till a comparatively late period.

8. Needless to say that signs of silver and gold are no strangers along the Queensland coast.

9. I have referred to the salmon and pig-fish, which are particularly referred to by De Quiros, but for which we search in vain at Santo. On the other hand, we find that the Queens-land rivers and coast abound with them. All visitors to Queensland are familiar with the pig-fish. As regards the salmon, an expert correspondent writes to me: "The most remarkable fresh-water fish in Queensland is the famous Burnett Salmon (ceratodus Forsteri). This salmon of De Quiros belongs to the Dipnoid fishes, of which there are only two other species in evidence, one in the Amazon, the other in South Africa. The existence of this fish in the (islands of the) South Seas is absolutely unknown to science." Mr. Stead, in.. "Fishes of Australia" (Sydney, 1906), refers to this particular species of salmon as frequenting the Burnett River, and also the Mary River, in Queensland.

10. Marble, and especially building marble, and limestone are abundant in Gladstone and its neighbourhood, and also in some of the islands off the harbour.

Seeing that the data furnished by the Spanish explorers fit in in such a singular manner with the Gladstone district and the Queensland coast, we feel justified in concluding that the Great Southern Land which was discovered by them was none other than our Australian Continent.

{Page 18}

IV.

Two arguments are advanced in favour of the Santo Island, which at first seem quite conclusive, but which, when more closely examined, are found to merit no attention.

1. The first argument is as follows:-The various narratives assign the Latitude 15 deg. 15 min. South as the exact position of the landing place in the newly discovered land. This leads us to Santo.

We must bear in mind, however, that in those days the maritime explorers in their published reports were careful to conceal the accurate latitude and longitude of the lands which they discovered, thus to lead astray their rival explorers and to prevent their appropriating the advantages of their discovery. This ruse of the early Spanish and Dutch navigators is referred to in the introduction to the first volume, of the Hakluyt series. Our own Australian Ernest Favenc, in his excellent "Story of Australian Exploration," p. 18 (Sydney, 1888), remarks that "the jealousy with which the maritime nations of Europe guarded their discoveries from each other has been the means of putting great difficulties in the way of tracing out the early traditions of the great South Land...

The generous emulation in the cause of scientific discovery was unknown, and the secrets of the sea were scrupulously kept."

Sir Clements Markham also remarks that "the Spanish Government jealously concealed the knowledge acquired by their great explorers" (I. xxviii.).

One of my critics has indeed remarked that though such jealousy prevailed in the early days of exploration, it had disappeared before the period of which we now treat. But it is quite the reverse. Never, perhaps, were the secrets of discovery more jealously guarded than at this very period.

In the narrative of his voyage, drawn up by his secretary but signed by himself, De Quiros adds, regarding his discovery (I. 157): "I beg you to keep it secret, for man does not know what time brings."

In the volumes just published by Sir Clements Markham we find (II., 516) a Memorial to the King of Spain accusing De Quiros of indiscretion in giving an account of his discoveries, "a proceeding which may cause serious inconvenience, from the information that foreigners way be able to gather, and thus send notices of those lands and of the navigation to their

{Page 19}

countrymen." The King on 31st October, 1610, with his own hand, gave the order: "Tell the same Quiros to collect these papers, and give them with secrecy to the officers of the Council of the Indies, for these things are not to pass through many hands."

2. The second argument is one on which our worthy citizen, Mr. Collingridge, and the secretary of the Geographical Society mainly rely. The map of the newly-discovered land, which was drawn by Diego de Prado y Tobar, and was for-warded by him to the Spanish. King from Goa on the 24th December, 1613, has at length come to light. It unmistakably presents to us the Santo Island.

I at once admit that this map of Prado y Tobar represents the Island of Santo, and I also admit that Prado y Tobar formed part of the expedition of De Quiros. Mr. Collingridge styles him the cartographer of the expedition, but of this high position there is no mention in the contemporary records. On the contrary, in two published lists (I., 254; IT., 382) he is assigned the office of storekeeper of the projected settlement, He pursued De Quiros with singular venom and undisguised hostility. De Torres, in his narrative, finds fault with De Quiros for his lenity in dealing with offenders. Only two members of his company had been punished by him during the voyage, and he only inflicted on them the trivial punishments of transferring them to his ship when they merited the gravest chastisement. One of these offenders was Prado y Tobar. All through De Quiros's subsequent career we find that this offender pursued him with unceasing enmity. Sr Clements Markham describes him as a mutinous officer, and again calls him the enemy, and the malignant enemy of De Quiros. (I., xvi., xxix., xxxii.).

Two letters of his are published by Sir C. Markham. They accompanied the map on which my critics now rely in these letters he calls De Quiros an impostor, a liar, and a fraud (II., 511, seqq.), who discovered nothing "but some reefs and small islands," and who should be wholly discredited in the statements of his Memorials and in his pretence to having found the great Austral Land. The map which he forwards is part and parcel of this attempt to discredit De Quiros. From the very outset similar attempts had been made. On his arrival in Mexico after his eventful voyage, De Quiros writes (I., 311)

{Page 20}

that "there were persons who, to gratify their evil passions, wrote to the Viceroy of Mexico, and sowed many letters all over the land, trying to misrepresent and discredit the expedition." So prejudiced were some members of the Council against him that he was, regarded "as a very dangerous man who might sell his knowledge and services to the English." (I., xxxv.).

That Santo was one of the islands discovered by De Quiros is unquestionable, and it is no less certain that the map forwarded from Goa in 1613 represents the Santo island; but when Prado y Tobar forwards the map of Santo as proof that the statements of the captain regarding his discovery of the great Austral Land were without foundation, I cannot but regard it as an additional argument in favour of my contention, that Santo cannot be the grand Austral continent of which De Quiros speaks and of which he claimed to be the discoverer.

V.

Some difficulties that have been urged against the claims of Port Curtis now demand our attention.

1. It has been remarked that some of the products commemorated by De Quiros, when he speaks of the "yams, oranges, limes, papans, almonds, nutmegs, mace, ginger and pepper," are not indigenous to the Queensland coast. We must bear in mind, however, that De Quiros refers to these as pro-ducts of the various islands and other lands which he had discovered, and not as characteristic of the territory around the harbour of Vera Cruz. The pioneers who explored the Port Curtis district in the middle of the last century found abundance of fruits among the natives. Mr. Friend, who was one of those explorers, writes to me that around Port Curtis "in the early days there were yams growing there and many kinds of wild fruits, even bread-fruit and wild bananas." Another expert attests that in the Gladstone district there are three varieties of the citrus, and that there is also a so-called wild plum (solanum) with a fine bloom on the fruit. A gentleman connected with the Department of Agriculture in Brisbane also writes: "As to indigenous fruits, the principal one is the Eugenia Myrtifolia, which bears a quantity of fruit. The Government Botanist here informs me that there are hundreds of these trees, and some settlers make the fruit into jam." All this

{Page 21}

harmonises perfectly with the accounts given by the Spanish explorers.

2. It has been argued, however, by Mr. Favenc that the explorers found in the land of their discovery a rich and fertile soil and all the requirements for a flourishing settlement. Now, he says, the territory around Port Curtis is the reverse of all this. He cites the words of Oxley, who, in 1823, having anchored in Port Curtis looking for a site for a convict settlement, reported to the Government as follows: "Having viewed and examined with the most anxious attention every point that afforded the least promise of being eligible for the site of a settlement, I respectfully submit it as my opinion that Port Curtis and its vicinity do not afford such a site; and I do not think that any convict establishment could be formed there that would return, either from the natural productions of the country or as arising from agricultural labour, any portion of the great expense that would necessarily attend its formation." It should be a sufficient reply to Mr. Oxley's report that he visited the country under very exceptional circumstances, and that the Government, as a matter of fact, ignored his report and proceeded to carry out the convict settlement which was projected there.

Another critic cites the testimony of "the Police Magistrate" at Gladstone, to the effect that, "speaking generally, there is not a decent piece of land around Port Curtis." This, indeed, would not be consistent with the statement of De Quiros that there was excellent land for every sort of cultivation in the district which he explored. However, it has been often remarked that Police Magistrates are not always the best or the most expert judges as regards the quality of land in their respective districts; and the present instance does not appear to be an exception to the rule. The editor of the "Gladstone Advocate," on February 16th, 1901, makes short work of the difficulty. He thus writes:

"It has been said that, speaking generally, there is not a decent piece of land around Gladstone. That, we think, is a question of horizon. If we limit our view to the town itself, and a few miles of its environments, the land is only reasonably good, with only patches of excellent quality. But if we take the Gladstone district generally such a statement is untrue. There is no finer land in Queensland-we might say Australia-than

{Page 22}

that which is to be found along the valleys of the Boyne and Calliope. It is marvellously rich and prolific, and suitable for agricultural or pastoral purposes. The close settlement which is now going on in the Gladstone district is proof of the excellent quality of the land."

In the earlier days of colonisation the same condition of the country was officially recognised, and I will cite one authority which cannot but be regarded as conclusive in this matter.

In the "Narrative of the Voyage of H.M.S. Rattlesnake," by Macgillivray' (published under the sanction of the Lords Commissioners of the Admiralty, London, 1852), is inserted an extract from a despatch of Colonel Barney, under date, Sydney, 20th July, 1847, relative to a proposed settlement at Gladstone (p. 52):

"The extent of land fit for agriculture, within a few miles of the coast, far exceeds the expectations I had formed on my first visit. Timber for dwelling-houses and for ship-building is abundant and of the best description; and within five miles of South Shore Head (the best site for a settlement) there is to be found pipe-clay, brick-earth, ironstone, freestone, granite, trap, slate, indications of coal; and, independent of a great sup-ply of shells for lime on the immediate site, there is at the head of one of the navigable salt creeks a fine freshwater stream running over a bed of limestone...The position and extent of Port Curtis, which I take to be the third harbour in importance in these seas, inferior only to Port Jackson and Hobart Town, must shortly lead to an establishment on its shore...The country is capable of affording all the tropical as well as a considerable portion of European produce, and will be found highly favourable for the breeding of stock."

3. De Quiros, in his Memorials to the King, refers specifically to one feature of the newly-discovered land which finds no counterpart in Santo or the other islands of the New Hebrides Group, but which is fully realised on the shores of Port Curtis. This is "the marble quarries," from which (as De Quiros adds) "sumptuous and elegant edifices could br, raised." Now, the most sanguine champions of Santo have not as yet found the slightest trace of marble there, whilst immense beds of marble crop up to the surface along the coast and in the islands off the coast at Port Curtis.

{Page 23}

As this is such a distinctive feature of the explored territory around the harbour of Vera Cruz, it may be well to recall a few passages that refer to it.

In a village that the explorers visited they found "a flute, and certain small things worked out of pieces of marble and jasper." Again, De Quiros writes: "It appeared to us that we saw there quarries of good marble; 1 say good, because several things were seen that were made of it and of jasper."

Of the natives it is said: "They work stone marble and make flutes, etc."

And again we read: "The convenience of such excellent soil, black, thick, and close, is that tiles and bricks may be manufactured. This, combined with good quarries, will enable large and sumptuous edifices to be built, the great abundance of timber giving help. Many mills can be erected, the rivers having such volume...The stone is fine, hard, and takes a polish. There are also very good quarries as in Madrid."

Some of my critics have endeavoured to lessen the weight of this argument by stating that the Gladstone marble is of inferior quality, "As to the marble or limestone deposits (one writer states), there is any quantity of it 14 miles from Glad-stone, but it is not good as a rule, having too much lime scattered through it. It is useless for mantelpieces, headstones, statues, etc." Here, however, it is to be remarked that it is of marble for building purposes that De Quiros speaks, and the more lime the marble may have the better will it suit for such purposes. All the marble quarries, however, in the Glad-stone district are not of the same quality. One of them is known by the name of Carrara, and has veins of the best quality of marble. An article in the "Gladstone Advocate," under date February the 16th, 1901, sets all difficulties at rest on this head, and proves to conviction that in so far as this feature of the discovered land is concerned, it harmonises perfectly with the Port Gladstone district. It is as follows:

"It will be noticed that the existence of marble is not denied. But that it is of an inferior quality we utterly refute. We have frequently referred to the marble deposits of this district. It is true that the deposits which form the bed and steep bank of the Calliope River are inferior to deposits found in other parts of the district, being, for the most part, a breccia marble, the particles being fastened with an iron cement,

{Page 24}

but it takes a beautiful polish and has a most variegated appearance. These deposits are easily reached by way of the river, The Calliope River crossing is paved with marble. There are also large deposits on the Boyne River. But the locality is rich in all varieties of this classic stone, from white statuary marble almost equal to the finest Carrara, and the blackest of black marbles, to the most variegated. It is not confined to one spot, but abounds throughout the whole district. That it is of good quality, and could be utilised for building, ornamental or statuary purposes, we can aver, as we speak with some degree of experience, and have before us as we write polished samples of almost every description to be found in the district. That it can be used to good purpose may be seen at any time if one likes to examine the marble font in the Presbyterian Church, which is made from local marble. The mantelpieces in the Queensland Parliament House are also made from marble from the Gladstone district. A table made from our marble was sent to the Paris Exhibition, and the maker was awarded a silver medal. There are also monuments and tombstones in our local cemetery. There are polished tablets which have been exposed to the weather since 1858 as good in appearance now as they were then, Samples of the marble and many ornaments made from it were sent to the Indian and Colonial Exhibition in 1886, and the exhibitor was

awarded a certificate and a medal. This is proof enough, surely, of its quality. If De Quiros or any other navigator sailed up the Calliope River, the mouth of which is a couple of miles north of Auckland Inlet, on which Gladstone stands, he could not miss the marble deposits there, but he might easily be pardoned if he did not ascertain if there was any-thing of a superior quality some distance away, or inquire into its quality. The mere fact that there was marble would probably be sufficient information for him."

4. Another common difficulty against the opinion which I have adopted recalls to mind the fact that hitherto every writer on the geography of the South Seas has regarded Santo as the Great Southern Land discovered by De Quiros. It cannot but be presumptuous, it is said, to advance an opinion contrary to such a consensus of expert writers. Findlay, however, has well remarked that in this matter geographers have, as a matter of course, accepted without inquiry the statements of Captain

{Page 25}

Cook. He found that the degree of latitude assigned by De Quiros harmonised with Santo, and he at once accepted its big bay as the landing place of the great Spanish explorer. Probably not one of the subsequent geographical writers knew anything of Santo except what was set forth by Captain Cook, for the New Hebrides were outside the ordinary track of navigation, and were but little known till our own day; and, on the other hand, the original sources of information regarding the discovery of De Quiros were not available. The mountains of the Moon bordering on the Sahara in Africa present a similar instance. A traveller some 200 years ago having referred to such a chain of mountains, each subsequent geographer assigned them their due position in the African Continent. When Stanley penetrated Central Africa, no such mountain range could be found, and it at once became evident that they were mere moonshine. The identifying Santo with the Great Southern Land was no less a delusion.

It is not accurate, however, to state that all geographers have hitherto been agreed in assigning Santo as the Great Land discovered by De Quiros. Our worthy Sydney citizen, Mr. Collingridge (p. 305), reproduces the map of that Southern Land published in 1752 by the geographer to the King of France, who manifestly had access to original sources not generally available. His map presents a fair outline of our Australian Continent, and on its North-East coast, pretty well corresponding to the position of Port Curtis, he marks the harbour of Vera Cruz, discovered by De Quiros.

5. Some critics have remarked that although the Boyne of the Queensland coast is a fair-sized river, yet it can have no claim to be likened to the Guadalquivir (the very name of which implies a "great river"), which for 60 miles of its course to the city of Seville is navigable for the largest vessels. But we must attend to the words of De Quiros. He expressly states that the river which he discovered was as large as the Guadalquivir at Seville, that is, 60 miles from its mouth. Beyond Seville, the Guadalquivir is navigable only for smaller craft and little frigates. The Boyne may justly be compared to it at that stage of its course.

6. It only remains to consider the difficulty advanced by Mr. Ernest Favenc, who, writing in the "Australian Journal of Education" (September 1st, 1904), contends that the data furnished

{Page 26}

by De Torres are irreconcilable with the claim of Port Curtis. De Torres (he says) sailed from the newly-discovered harbour of Vera Cruz on a south-westerly course till he reached the 27 deg. of S. latitude, and then, veering his course to the N.W., came upon the southern coast of New Guinea, and discovered the Strait that bears his name. If we suppose him to start from Port Curtis on such a course, he must have sailed through the Australian Continent. In this statement of the case, however, it seems to me that Mr. Favenc does not do justice to the genuine meaning of De Torres's narrative. I interpret him to imply that he resolved to continue the voyage where De Quiros had interrupted it at the 26 deg. South latitude, thus to carry out what he believed to be the royal instructions. According to this interpretation, he sailed some days along the Queensland coast, but finding the winds unfavourable, proceeded to the latitude and longitude where. De Quiros had abandoned the southern voyage. Thence De Torres sailed towards the south to the 30 deg., and even passed that latitude one degree on a south-east course. This would bring him approximately to the longitude 163 deg. as marked on our maps. Finding no land, he directed his course to the north-west, where eventually he fell in with the southern coast of New Guinea. This appears to be the natural meaning of the words of De Torres, and the course of navigation which he would thus have pursued is quite reconcilable with the fact that Fort Curtis was his starting point. Mr. Collingridge (p. 234) calls attention to the fact that De Torres speaks of the "mentioned latitude" and the "said latitude" in a mysterious way, and remarks that the accurate latitude "was, no doubt, purposely kept secret."

There is one feature of Mr. Favenc's diagram which it will be well to bear in mind. He allows De Torres to proceed only to about the 27 deg. on Ms S.W. course from Santo, and then marks out his N.W. course to New Guinea. But De Torres's statement must be our guide in marking out the course which he pursued, and he tells us that he sailed S.W. till he reached the 31 deg. S. latitude. Now, following out the diagram of Mr. Favenc, this course would inevitably lead him to the Australian mainland.

7. Someone perhaps will say that there are far more than seven islands lying off the coast of Keppel Bay. De Quiros,

{Page 27}

however, states: "At this port and bay are many excellent islands, seven of which may be especially mentioned" Compare this with Findlay's account of the Keppel Bay coast (p. 983). There is, he tells us, the Capricorn group with three principal islands; then the Bunker group, also with three islands. These "occupy an extent of 54 miles nearly parallel with the coast." Then comes Curtis Island, 25 miles in length. All these form as if the outer barrier of the magnificent bay.

Bermudez further remarks that these seven islands are "in sight of the port;" and that "nearly half-way there are other known islands," All this is verified at Port Curtis, for Facing Island, eight miles in length, and other smaller islands stand midway between the port and Curtis Island, and thus all details admirably fit in with the description given in the Spanish narratives.

8. There remains one serious difficulty which affects, not the territory, but the natives of the discovered, land. The various narratives reckon the bow and arrow and wooden swords among their weapons of war. Such weapons, however, were unknown to the Queensland aboriginals when the territory was visited by Captain Cook and subsequent explorers.

To this difficulty the distinguished Victorian geographer, Mr. Panton to whom i have already referred has replied that the Spaniards might easily have mistaken for arrows some of the spears which are still in use among our aboriginals. Ile writes: "Anyone who has ever seen a sheaf of reed spears would look upon them as large arrows. The natives can throw them some 200 yards, and they might very easily be mistaken for arrows by Spaniards seeing them for the first time." This specially holds good when the natives make use of the spear-rest. The same writer adds: As to wooden swords, 1 would ask: Has anyone seen such a weapon in Santo? In Australia some weapons do resemble swords. 1 have several in my collection."

We may further remark, however, that those who have made a study of, our 'aboriginals have come to the conclusion that more than one wave of invasion from the Java and the Malay Peninsula must have swept over parts of Australia. In-dependent even of this; we may readily suppose that during the 200 years that elapsed between the discovery of De Quiros and the British occupation of Australia, many unrecorded vicissitudes may live occurred. The tribes from the mountains may

{Page 28}

have pressed upon the natives inhabiting the coast and compelled them to take refuge in the islands scattered through-out the Torres Strait and in New Guinea. In these islands the bow and arrow have long been in constant use. Macgillivray, in "Voyage of the Rattlesnake"(p. 296), when engaged in the exploration of the Islands of Torres Straits off Cape York, writes that the natives there "readily parted with the bows and arrows, of which they had a very large supply." With the vicissitudes of the natives, however, we are not primarily dealing at present. We are considering the unchanging features of the land discovered by De Quiros. These are inconsistent with the island of Santo, and are found to harmonise satisfactorily with Port Curtis and the adjacent Queensland territory.

VI.

De Quiros had won his laurels as an explorer in the islands of the Pacific towards the close of the 16th century. And now one grand project engrossed his thoughts. He would discover the Great Southern Land, and would rival the glory of Columbus by bringing new nations under the salutary influence of religion. But how could he secure the approval of the Spanish Government for a scheme which to many seemed visionary and elusive?

It was the Jubilee year, 1600. Pilgrims from every part of Europe were flocking to Rome. He, too, would take the pilgrim's staff, and whilst in Rome he might perhaps enlist the Pontiff's sympathy for his enterprise.

In the volumes of the Hakluyt Society now published by Sir Clements Markham (London, 1904) we have from De Quiros himself the narrative of his pilgrimage. He landed in the month of August, 1600, in the territory of Genoa, and thence, "dressed as a pilgrim," traversed on foot several of the finest cities of Italy, where he remarks, "there was much to see and to notice."

Arriving in Rome, he was well received by the Spanish Ambassador. On the 28th of August he partook of the mid-day meal with the boor pilgrims, and in the afternoon had an audience of the Pontiff, Clement VIII., who listened attentively to his plans and commended his zeal and earnestness.

The most eminent astronomers and geographers in the Eternal City were invited to consider the project of De Quiros. In those days, as in later times, the most learned scientists

{Page 29}

of Europe made Rome their home. Among them was the German, Christopher Clavius, who taught mathematics in Rome for 20 years and was employed by Pope Gregory XIII. in the correction of the Calendar. He, with Toribio Perez, who had taught geography at Salamanca, and the learned Jesuit Villapando and others, examined and approved the project of De Quiros. As a result, Clement VIII. gave him commendatory letters for the Spanish Monarch, and granted many privileges and indulgences to those who would engage in his enterprise. De Quiros refers particularly to a particle of the wood of the Cross which was given to him by His Holiness, but which, he tells us, he obtained with very great difficulty. Sir C. Markham writes that the Pope's influence secured his success. Within a year he had obtained a royal order, through the Council of State, addressed to the Viceroy of Peru, instructing that dignitary to fit out two ships at Callao, to enable Quiros to undertake an expedition for the discovery of the Antarctic Continent."

Many difficulties, however, had yet to be overcome, and it was not till the month of December, 1605, that two ships and a zabra, or launch, were consigned at Callao to De Quiros for his glorious enterprise. The ship chosen for the captain him-self was named San Pedro y Sari Pablo, and was of 150 tons. The second ship was named San Pedro, 120 tons. The launch was named Los Tres Reyes.

With the details of the voyage we are not now concerned. Suffice it to say that on the 1st of May, in 1606, they entered a magnificent bay, and spread out before them was what De Quiros believed to be the grand continent of which he was in search. Two days later, as they sailed down the bay, they discovered a safe port in which a thousand ships could find anchorage. It was situated between two rivers, which supplied them with delicious fresh water, and they called it the port of Vera Cruz, from the feast of Holy Cross on which it was discovered. On the following days the coasts were explored, and the captain used every effort, but in vain, to engage in friendly relations with the natives.

Pentecost Sunday (10th May) was now at hand. On the eve all was joy and festivity on board the vessels, for next day would witness the solemn taking possession of the newly discovered land. A special order of Knights of the Holy Ghost

{Page 30}

was instituted in honour of the event. The camp master and an armed party attended to the preparations on shore. A small fort was equipped with four pieces of cannon. A temporary church was dedicated, under the invocation of Our Lady of Loreto, and in it an altar with a canopy was erected, adorned with palm branches and flowers. Masses were said at an early hour, and the whole expedition, officers and men, approached Holy Communion with the intent of gaining the Jubilee Indulgence granted them by Pope Clement VIII, High Mass was sung by the Father Commissary.

Two special facts are commemorated. The Father Commissary and his five Franciscan companions, barefooted and kneeling on the beach, received, at the hands of De Torres, the second in command, a large cross, "made of the orange wood of the country," in which was inserted the Relic of Holy Cross which the captain had received in Rome. This was borne aloft and all in procession, singing the "Lignum Crucis," advanced to. the church door, where the cross, with all solemnity, was set in a pedestal, and the captain announced in six distinct proclamations his taking possession of the newly-discovered land in the name of the Catholic Church, in the name of His Majesty the King, etc.

The second event was at the close of the High Mass. I. will describe it in the words of De Quiros's secretary: "The three ensigns, who now held the banners in their hands, inclined them to the ground in front of the altar, the Royal En-sign holding the royal standard. The Commissary blessed them with great solemnity; and at a certain signal that was given to the ships, whose mast-head banners displayed the Royal Arms and at the sides the two columns (symbols of the Spanish power) and the plus ultra, with the streamers fluttering;

fired off all their guns with full charges; the soldiers discharged muskets and arquebuses, and the gunners sent off rockets and fire-wheels. In the middle of al-l this noise, all shouted with almost infinite joy, and many times, Long Live the Faith of Christ. And with this the celebration of the festival came to an end."

The next care of De Quiros was to institute and inaugurate a municipality to control the destinies of the future city. It is pleasing to find among the appointed magistrates a name which at the present day is highly honoured throughout Queensland, Julian Real.

{Page 31}

The festival of Corpus Christi was kept with due solemnity on the 21st of May. It was regarded by the Spaniards as "the first festival celebrated in honour of the Most High Lord iii these strange and unknown lands."

The secretary of De Quiros gives a minute and detailed description of this beautiful feast.

On the 20th of May the camp master, with a hundred soldiers, went on shore to adorn the church, and to mark our the streets for the procession. Before daybreak on the 21st all were ashore. The church was "bravely decorated" with green branches. The altar in particular was richly ornamented; a large oil-painting of the Crucifixion served as the altar-piece, the candles were lighted and the incense burning.

There were three high triumphal arches, enlaced with palms, branches of fruit trees and flowers; the ground was also strewn with flowers. The streets were formed with a variety of trees, and at two angles, under two other arches, were erected two altars of repose with their canopies; on these altars were the images of St. Peter and St. Paul.

In the Church three Masses were celebrated. The day was clear and serene, and as the sun rose over the crowns of the trees, its rays entering through the branches, the difference in the fruits of each plant was shown in great profusion. Here, too, could be heard the persistence with which the birds sang and chanted; the leaves and branches were seen to move gently, and the whole place was agreeable, fresh, shady, with a gentle air moving, and the sea smooth."

The order of procession is minutely described. A soldier went first, holding aloft the heavy cross of orange wood. Next came a lay brother bearing a gilt cross, attended by Acolytes and Thurifer, all wearing red cassocks and surplices. Then followed the three companies in order, each one bearing its banner in the centre; with its drums sounding a march. As was usual in the Spanish processions, there was a picturesque sword-dance by eleven sailor lads, dressed in red and green silk, with bells on their feet. "They danced with much dexterity and grace, to the sound of a guitar, which was played by a respected old sailor." This was followed by another dance per-formed "by eight boys, all dressed like Indians in shirts and breeches of silk, coloured brown, blue, and grey, with garlands on their heads and white palms in their hands. Bands of bells

{Page 32}

were around their ankles, and they danced with very quiet countenances, at the same time singing their canticles to the sound of tambourines and flutes played by two musicians."

Six Magistrates preceded the Celebrant, each with a lighted torch in his hand. The Father Commissary, attended by the other Priests, officiated; the canopy of yellow silk, six yards long, was borne by three royal officers and three Magistrates; and the "Pange Lingua" was joyfully sung. After the canopy the Royal Standard was borne by the Ensign, attended by two, Justices of the Peace and the chief constable.

As soon as the canopy appeared outside the church "all the bells rang, and the people who were looking on attentively fell on their knees; the Ensigns lowered the banners three times, the drummers beat the drums for battle; the soldiers, who had the cords ready, fired off the muskets and arquebuses; the constables fired off the guns which were on shore for defending the port; and in the ships the artillerymen fired off the bombards and pieces, and those placed in the launch and boats for the occasion. Once more, and once again, they were discharged. When the smoke cleared away, there were seen amongst the green branches so many plumes of feathers and sashes, so many pikes, halberds, javelins, bright sword-blades, spears, lances, and on the breasts so many crosses and so much gold, and so many colours and silken dresses, that many eyes could not contain what sprung from the heart, and they shed tears of joy. With this the procession returned, the church being guarded by four corps de garde. The dancers kept dancing to keep up the festival, and remained within; and the captain at the door said to them: "All the dresses you wear, you can keep as your own, for they are from the Royal Treasury; I would that they were of the best and richest brocade.""

To bring the ceremonies to a close a fourth Mass was said to satisfy the devotion of the sentries "who were posted to keep a look-out for any approach of the natives, though they were far off on the beach and on the hills."

The narrative adds that, "having given the soul such sweet and delicious food," the tables were now laid under the shade of tall and spreading trees, where all were gladdened with a welcome and joyous repast.

Thus were brought to a close the first festive celebrations which marked the discovery of our Australian Continent.

Title:	Discovery of Australia by de Quiros in the Year 1606
Author:	Patrick F. Cardinal Moran, Archbishop of Sydney.
	* A Project Gutenberg of Australia eBook *
eBook No.:	0600641h.html

This eBook was produced by: Col Choat and Bob orsyth"[1]

Appendix 2

GODDARD'S SECTION WITHIN CHAPTER 6:
"WORDS ON THE ROCKS" BY ROY GODDARD

CERTAIN OBSERVATIONS ON ABORIGINAL ROCK CARVINGS IN THE WOLLOMBI DISTRICT, NEW SOUTH WALES.

BY

R. H. GODDARD.

[Abstract]

"The almost total absence of historical facts, relative to the aborigine of Australia, during the long ages that have passed since the continent was first peopled until the advent of the white man precludes the possibility of any satisfactory data upon which to trace their ancestry. We are therefore compelled to fall back upon the rock sculptures, cave paintings, and the language for the solution of the problem.

It is frequently felt that many of the sculptures and paint ings of the Australian aborigine must have been executed with the intention of exercising an influence upon the minds of the aborigine: teaching the younger men to maintain traditional relationships and modes of conduct, in fact a religion, that bound them into closer unity and sound organisation.(1)

The late Mrs. Rachel Milson as late as 1910 used to relate tales of the aborigines of the Wollombi District, who from time to time would leave their women and children camped down by the river and go off into the Devil Mountain " to be made men."

Some years ago Mr. Walter Enright gave it as his opinion that the Devil Mountain in the Wollombi District, possibly referred to Devil's Rock, or Burragurra, in the Parish of Burra gurra, County of Northumberland, District of Windsor, N.S.W. This is a flat sandstone cap on a spur of the main dividing range between the Macdonald and the Wollombi. I therefore decided to investigate this area, and, accompanied by Mr. Enright and Mr. Carlyle Greenwell, we undertook an expedition to Burragurra early in August, 1935. Few persons ever visit this spot,

---

(1). Elkin's work on the Ungarinyn Tribe--Proc. Roy. Soc. N.S.W., LXIX, p. 206, Love's work on the Warora Tribes of West Australia - Proc. A.N.Z.A.A.S., XXII, p. 227, Wood-Jones on the ordered arrangement of stones present in certain parts of Australia-Proc. Roy. Anl. Inst., LXL, '25, and Spencer and Gillan, and Howitt 's, all indicate that there was much more in these relics than we have assumed in the past-Proc. A.A.A.S., VI, p. 147.

Page 2

unless it is to hunt up straying cattle, and then the approach would be via Blaxland 's Line, an almost forgotten road from the township of St. Albans-following the ridges to Fordwich. The aborigine probably made use of this track to go to and from this Ceremonial Ground at Burragurra long before John Blaxland formed Fordwich Station on the 8th March, 1831.

Accompanied by Matthew Denne as guide, our approach was from Mogo Creek, a rough climb of about 1,000 feet for four miles to the West, until we met Blaxland 's Line. (2) Following this in a northerly direction, we kept to the main ridges. At about six mile from Mogo Creek two large carvings of emu pads, as if travelling north, were observed, the measurements being six inches across the pad and eight inches to the centre spur. These pads are three feet apart and the grooving is one inch deep. Six inches to the North is a raised circular knob twelve inches in diameter; the knob is surrounded by a vein of iron forming the lip, and its centre is a kind of quartzite rock. Considerable weathering of the surrounding rock has left this knob elevated about five inches.

About a mile further up this ridge the track passes in a northerly direction across another sandstone outcrop, sloping away to the S.W. In the centre we observed two natural pot holes eight inches apart and almost circular, that on the western extremity measuring eighteen inches in diameter and four feet deep. On the lower edge were several lines.(3) It is postulated that these linemarkings or grooves would be made by the aborigines in grinding their stone axes, and from their position the markings appear to have some particular significance in respect to the water here.(4)

Two wavy lines or troughs have been cut in the upper side the familiar sign of the Karia - forming this pot-hole, and measuring twelve feet and fourteen feet respectively. (Plate I.) The second pot-hole, being the more easterly one, measured two feet in diameter and is twelve inches deep.

Mr. Enright informed us that he had it on the authority of Mr. Elliot, of Buttai, that the aborigine of this district in the early days had an intoxicating drink, made of wild honey and

---

(2). Ref. R. 841 Map, Land Titles Office.

(3). Mountford-Proc. A.N.Z.A.A.S., XXII, p. 212.

(4). E. Giles, in his Journal of Explorations in Central Australia-Proc. A.A.A.S., VI, ·p. 138, mentions a drawing depicting a snake with its head apparently in a rock-hole, possibly having ceremonial significance-Collyboi, the guardian of waterholes.

Page 3

water, that was called Bool, and was drunk by the Karaji(5) in their ceremonies.

On further examination of this area the initials J.B. were discovered carved in the rock, and evidently of considerable age.

It was conjectured that, as this track had been used by Blaxland in the early part of last century, it was quite possible the initials referred to John Blaxland, of Fordwich. This natural catchment had been improved by deepening with metal tools.

This was the only water we found during the day, and would in all probability be preserved by those early pioneers to refresh both man and beast on their travels to and fro.

At approximately eight miles from Mogo Creek, at the end of a spur of the range branching away to the West of Blaxland 's Line, there appears a flat sandstone rock about an acre in extent, towering above the surrounding country. This is the Devil's Rock, or Burragurra. About five miles to the West is Yango Mountain, rising 3,345 feet above sea level, and beyond, a few points to the South-West, the Chimney Stack, or Tyan Peak, at Capertee can be discerned. Mount Werong is to the North, and beyond is Mount Merwin, or Howe's Mount.

There are some remarkable carvings depicted on Devil's Rock, but owing to the heavy snow clouds hanging about it was not easy to discern them at first. Fortunately there was a break in the clouds for a short period, and with the lengthening rays of the sun the carvings showed up in sharp relief, long enough for us to make our records.

Our observation confirmed the stories which we had heard of the Devil's Rock-that it was an aboriginal Bora ground, where the Karaji carried out their ceremonies in connection with initiation into manhood.(6) There was no doubt as to the meaning of the carvings found. These carvings include an arrangement of several figures of men and animals, mundowa and emu tracks leading from one station to another.

Approaching from the East to West we observed the carvings of ten emu pads, each three feet apart, and leading to the first carved full-length figure, which has so weathered that its complete outline, apart from the trunk and snout, could not be traced. (Plate II.)

To the South is a group of carved emu tracks and foot pads

---

(5). Karadjeri-Elkin-Oceania, Vol. VI, 2, p. 144.

(6). Enright-The Kattang-Jour. Anthrop. Soc. N.S.W., Vol. I, p. 75.

Page 4

surrounding a raised circular knob, similar to the one previously described. Three of these markings were joined together by a line running through them.

Two feet to the North-West of the figure first described is a carving, four feet in length, resembling a dog.

Four feet to the West is the first carving of three spirit pads, or mundowa, one inch deep, twelve inches long, and eight inches wide, travelling in a northerly direction ; these pads are also three feet apart.(7) The third pad forms part of another carving of a figure, measuring· five feet to extremities.

This last figure corresponds to Mulla Mulla, the spirit of darkness. Three feet West of the last figure is the most striking figure carved at Devil's Rock. Depicted in a sitting posture, with one arm outstretched to the North, it appears to have five eyes, and measures from the extremity of the foot to the upstretched hand four feet in length and is two feet three inches across. (Plate III.)

This figure probably represents the traditional Wa-boo-ee, the demon-spirit of the Wollombi tribe, who was supposed to have sprung from Devil's Rock and landed on Yango, in the West (Yango, or Yengo dilla, meaning '' caught by the foot," or '' step ping over"). Wa-boo-ee was of great stature-he thought nothing of stepping up to the sky for a change of residence and of throwing a few rocks, in the shape of mountains, down to the earth as stepping-stones. Wa-boo-ee controlled the seasons. Mr. Enright reports that he had it on good authority that there was also a mundowa carved on Yengo Mountain.

Heading away from the hand, towards the West, there are four more carvings of emu pads three feet apart. At seventeen feet distant there is another remarkable carving of a figure three feet six inches across. This figure has a curved snout and is in a squatting attitude; it appears to have three or four ears, or else the top "ear" depicts an emu pad carved at the apex.

Carvings of emu pads continue on beyond this figure across the whole face of the rock, the last emu pad being on an isolated rock in the scrub. These emu pads are also three feet apart and in line with Yengo Mountain.

At the third emu pad from this last-mentioned carving there is another carved emu track branching off at right angles and

---

(7). Kenyon-Art of the Australian Aborigine, p. 20.

Page 5

leading due North again. The carvings of eight emu pads were observed in this direction and were also placed three feet apart.

There is also yet another track of carvings leading away to the South-West from the outstretched hand of the figure representing Wa-boo-ee, forming four emu pads, three feet apart, to the carved figure of the traditional Moori-the spirit of life(8) - measuring four feet in length, with five rays spreading from his head, and with arms outstretched, as in the former figure.(9)

Three feet to the West is another carved figure two feet in length of the trunk, arms outstretched and fore-shortened legs.

Heading away to the South seven more emu pads were observed, also three feet apart. The most prominent rise in the ranges in this direction is Mount Wilson, with Mount Irvine just below its ridge. It might be mentioned here that there is a similar figure carved at Mount Irvine to the figure here depicted as Mulla Mulla already described.(10)

Reverting to Burragurra, there is, four feet to the NorthWest from the figure last described, a carving of a kangaroo, measuring three feet from head to tip of tail. Where normally the front paws should be there is carved what appears to be a bird's leg and claws.

In the centre of the triangle formed by Wa-boo-ee, Moori, and the figure in a squatting attitude there is a carving of the Muron or U-sign-meaning life.(11)

Eight feet from the "Kangaroo" West are two carved Circles twelve inches apart and each twenty-two inches in diameter. Three feet to the South of the Circles is a carved emu pad, five inches in length, leading to another carving of a remarkable figure two feet in width. (12) Owing to the disintegration of the rock, it is hard to discern the full outline, but the last figure resembles the figure first described in this paper.

Twelve inches further South is the carving of a short animal, which is probably representing a wombat. Six feet beyond are carvings of two more Circles, ten inches and eighteen inches in

---

(8). Slater-Aboriginal Literature, p. 2.

(9). Worship-referring to Sir George Grey's Journals of Expeditions in Australia-describes a figure-Proc. A.A.A.S., Vol. VI, p. 138: "Its head was encircled by bright red rays something like the rays one sees proceeding from the sun ... ' '

(10). Jour. Anthrop. Soc. N.S.W., Vol. I, pt. 10, p. 225.

(11). Described by Mountford in his survey of petroglyphs in South Australia-Proc. A.N.Z.A.A.S., XXII, p. 213.

(12). Kenyon-Art of the Australian Aborigine, p. 30.

Page 6

diameter respectively. The carving of a small snake, twelve inches long, is also depicted nearby, as if travelling towards the Circle.(13)

There are many other traces of carvings, but owing to the disintegration of the rock surface they could not be fully discerned, and, like most aboriginal rock carvings they are lost for all time.

The possibility of Yengo Mountain being a connecting link with this interesting ceremonial ground induced us to go there. Transport was our main problem; rough mountain ranges, such as we had to face, could only be covered by sure-footed horses, and after some trouble ,we managed to obtain a sufficient number of mounts to transport our gear, as well as ourselves, from the nearest point that could be reached by car.

We set out early on the 25th January, 1936, and upon reaching Cagney's Run, at Yango Creek, we loaded all our gear on the pack-horses and started upon our climb up on to the range towards Yango. Shortly after midday we reached Finchley Trigonometrical Station, where our guide showed us the direction of another spur of the range, branching off in a southerly direction towards Blaxland's Line and Burragurra, and at some distance along the spur there were aboriginal drawings upon the rocks. We decided, however, that we had better press forward if we desired to reach our first stage by nightfall and we left these carvings for our return journey. '

At last we began to descend from the range into the rich pastures of Big Yango Valley, and at 5 p.m. we reached Forbes Hut, which had been fixed as our base camp.

Our next stage was the real climb up to the top of Yengo Mountain. Starting out early, we followed up Mountain Creek, and once upon the spur our track was fairly even over sandstone ridges for five miles. Yengo is a volcanic cap, and half-way up the mountain we had to dismount and lead our horses over the rough, broken basalt slabs until we reached the summit.

The formation of the mountain is geologically of more recent origin than that of the other basaltic peaks in the surrounding country, where the rock has disintegrated, leaving a covering of rich volcanic soils. YeJ1go, on the other hand, is covered with broken basaltic slabs, which are not disintegrated, and these are most difficult to traverse, for nearly a thousand feet to the summit.

---

(13). Worsuop refers to carvings in the rock at Nandoo Creek, Central Queensland, of Emus' feet, snakes and boomerangs-Proc. A.A.A.S., VI, p. 143.

Page 7

On reaching the summit we then realised that this mountain had been wrongly indicated as the site of a mundowa. No trace of a carving or a mundowa could be found, the rock not being suitable for carving. The tradition that Wa-boo-ee had stepped on this mountain from Burragurra, and had left his footmark, could not be confirmed. Wa-boo-ee, who controlled the seasons, could also be represented by the Sun, and since this mountain is clue West of Burragurra, or the Devil's Rock, the tradition may have arisen from the fact that the Sun was always seen to dis appear behind Yengo Mountain from the Devil's Rock.

After taking our bearings and exploring the top of the mountain, we began our descent, a task which proved even more difficult than the ascent, on account of the loose stones underfoot for our horses. Eventually we reached our camp well after dusk.

Our plans for the next day were discussed, and it was decided that by getting an early start we would be able to reach the Rock Carvings at the head of Yango in the day.

Breaking camp at dawn, we were soon in the saddle and well on our way before the heat of the day. The turn off on the track at Finchley, leading to the Rock Carvings, was reached about noon, and, riding along the top of the ridge separating the head waters of the Yango Creek and a branch of the Macdonald River, we came quite suddenly upon a circular clearing of level land surrounded by low scrub at the edge of a sandstone spur of the range.

This appeared to be an old Bora ground, where the aborigines assembled for their ceremonies, the rock carvings being just beyond. The first carvings observed were two full-length emus, with a pathway between them, leading from the circular clearing to the main carvings on the smaller enclosure. These figures measured five feet from head to tail and one foot eight inches across the back. (Plate IV.)

Fifty feet to the South-East is a carving of a figure similar to that of Moori at Burragurra, with rays spreading up from the head ; but in this figure there are eight rays instead of five ; further, there are two boomerangs, one above the right hand, the other at the left foot, which do not appear at Burragurra.

This figure also has five eyes and something which appears to be a girdle round the waist ; the length of the figure is eight feet. Twenty feet due South is a carving of a similar figure five feet long by one foot wide holding a boomerang in the right hand but without any rays spreading from the head. Touching its left

Page 8

hand is a carving of another of these figures and continuing in a semi-circle for four feet is a carving of a similar figure measuring six feet in length by four feet in width.

The last figure appears to be lying across a coolimon or a shield. Two other similar figures complete a semi-circle. Continuing what appears to be the other half of a complete circumference in the intervening space before we reach the first figure there appear a line here and a line there; but the rock has weathered considerably and any figures that may have been carved here to complete the circle have almost disappeared. The carvings of three emu pads lead away to the South South-East in the direction of Burragurra and at approximately fifty feet to the East is a circle of one foot eight inches in diameter cut in the rock.(14)

There are several other carvings, but, unfortunately, the weathering has so obliterated them that they cannot be followed except the form of a kangaroo, the outline of which follows the contour of the rock surface and is seen in bold relief.

Mr. Enright put forward the theory that possibly this ceremonial ground which is undoubtedly much older than that at Burragarra, w s abandoned at the beginning of the white occupation in this neighbourhood in favour of Burragurra, a more remote and secluded location for the instruction and practice in their rites. It was also within easy distance of the Wollombi meaning "the meeting." Mitchell mapped this district as Corob-ere.(15)

The established trade routes from the North and North-West traversed this part of the country, a part of the Comilroy, the boundaries of which appear to be involved somewhat in obscurity, different writers describing the boundaries differently.

Breton describes an aboriginal fight which took place at the Wollombi in which the Comileroy blacks were engaged.(16)

The Wailalun, adjoining to the West, spoke a language understood by both the Comilroy and the Wailalun ; they also

---

(14). In the Macdonnell Ranges there is a rock shelter depicting the rising sun emu's feet branches of acacia, the usual snake, and a wheel-like sign Proc. A.A.A.S., p. 140. At Ooraminna rock-hole, on the overland telegraph line, there are sketches of emu's feet, snakes and other mythical drawings Proc. A.A.A.S., VI, p. 141.

(15). Sir Thomas L. Mitchell's Survey of July, 1829-R.841.L.T.O.

(16). Lieut. Breton-Excursions in New South Wales-London-1833.

Page 9

preserved the old words and traditions that had been handed down.(17)

The geological formation of the surrounding country also shows this route as the natural one that would be taken by those passing to and fro to trade, maintaining relationships between different groups, joining in ceremonies or settling hostilities.

Blaxland, in his search for a track through to Fordwich as an alternative to the sea journey, via Newcastle and the Hunter River, would, it is submitted, be led by a native, who, naturally, going into strange country, would take the trade route in preference to going across unknown and possibly hostile country. Mitchell, in his explorations through to the North, would travel with his native guide along this aboriginal trade route into Queensland.(17) By checking his tracks and the existing stock routes running through to the Gulf Country from this district one can easily recognise the old trade route ·which followed up and down the river, even to the far North-West of the Continent.

Coomilroi, Wolroi, Gunnebal and Giroombul tribes (18) were known to pass up the Namoi ; and likewise the Wailalun, the Castlereagh, to the Wollombi and Howe's Valley for certain ceremonies in which the several groups would assemble. Hence, we have these traditional sacred grounds with their "permanent records," ideographs and venerated objects. The Karaji could read any "permanent records" into his own spoken dialect and two tribes might well express the same symbol by totally different syllables, but all would interpret the symbol by the same or similar concepts. Symbols would teach the initiate, maybe, that there was a Supreme Being, that there were subordinate spirits both good and evil. The symbols could depict a lesson of a creation, or that of life and death, and his own relation to the Supreme Being. He might, perhaps, mix up his primitive tenets with many imaginings, but by natural persuasion his faith in the existence of Goel was ineradicable.

Burragurra to the aboriginal was as Glastonbury to Medieval England.

---

(17). Mitchell's Despatches of 1846.
(18). Macpherson-Proc. Linn. Soc. N.S. Wales, 1904(4), Pt. II.[1]

Appendix 3

JON WYATT'S EMAIL TO STEVEN ON SLATER'S "THE NEWSPAPERS"

Hi Steven,

here are my suggested changes to what I think is an important article of record.

The Newspapers

In about 1895, Frederic Salter while still in his mid twenties, became managing editor of the Gulgong Advertiser. From about 1898 he was founding editor of the Gladstone Advocate. From about 1902 he headed the Charters Towers Evening Telegraph where he remained for several years. In about 1912 he moved to Sydney and worked for the Sydney Sun. From 1921 to 1924 he managed the Newcastle Sun where he increased circulation; he then returned to the Sydney Sun, the parent newspaper. In subsequent years, Slater published a plethora of feature articles, opinion pieces and letters in practically all the Sydney newspapers, including the Sydney Morning Herald, Sydney Mail and Daily Telegraph. His stories were also reprinted in country newspapers. He also wrote a regular column 'Sydney Topics' for the Melbourne Age. It's fair to say he was read from Rockhampton to Melbourne and beyond. Slater was no angel with the pen and was very sarcastic with people he disagreed with.

Literary Works

In 1897, while at Gulgong, he self published his book of poems *Sea Foam and Passion Flowers and* this was well received; the National Library Canberra and the Mitchell Library both have a copy. While at Charters Towers he self published the two comedic operas .... and major libraries hold a copies of those. He also serialised 3-4 of his novels in the Charters Towers Telegraph, including 'Sins of the Fathers' 1903 an Australian Romance; and 'Blood of the Ghettos' 1907 under the nom de plume "Don Fredrigo" a futurtistic horror story. For some reason, publishing houses never printed his fiction.

Cardinal Moran

In 1895 Cardinal Moran published the tome 'History of the Catholic Church, from Authentic Sources' in which he claimed descriptions of a harbour by Quiros fitted Port Curtis not the

New Hebrides. The Spanish government routinely published false co-ordinates of newly discovered lands to mislead rival nations, and the King of Spain only knew the true co-ordinates, thus the confusion.

Slater while managing the Gladstone Advocate, interviewed many local old timers who mentioned seeing Spanish relics in the area, such as a rock carving of a face, 2-3 ancient wells, an altar stone, three canons, an ancient ship's hulk... the relics had since 'disappeared', but Slater remained convinced these people were telling the truth.

In 1909, Cardinal Moran published 'Discovery of Australia by de Quiros in the Year 1606', to silence the many critics of his first book. In this he quotes the "editor of the Gladstone Advocate", regarding soil fertility and marble deposits in the Gladstone area. In 1909 Slater was at Charters Towers but Moran had apparently consulted with him some years before while preparing the book.

Steven, I think the title of the article is most apt, Slater reported the evidence as he saw it and 'stuck to his guns' even when it was an inconvenient truth.

I've unearthed a few other details about Slater and the family and I'll pass those after this article is bedded down.

Hope this helps.

Jon Wyatt.[1]

Other Books:

*INTERVIEW WITH AN ALIEN BY STEVEN STRONG & LEA KAPITELI

Every month for the past year, Steven Strong has given Mezreth a list of questions to provide his take on humans, Earth, life, and the greater universe. Though not technically, Lea Kapiteli is the mediator for the answers, providing context to the ribbons of thoughts and concepts that wrap into our linear and limited language.

"If I was to offer the impossible, to be able to speak to the Creator of Everything, and ask anything you want, surely only a fool would decline. But what if the next-in-line was willing and able to tell you everything, would you be agreeable to have a series of conversations?" Steven Strong.

"Mezreth only talks to people who listen, but once he starts, he never shuts up." Lea.

Through Amazon:
https://www.amazon.com/Interview-Alien-Lea-Kapiteli/dp/064867732X

Through Authors (Paperback) Signed (Australian Customers):
https://www.ouralienancestry.net/product-page/interview-with-an-alien

Through Authors (eBook):

https://www.ouralienancestry.net/product-page/interview-with-an-alien-1

"Interview with an Alien is a compendium of images of some of these intelligence's Lea has interacted and communicated with. However, the specific communication with 'intelligence' Mezreth, is fascinating as he is a representative of an interstellar co-operative of many species. Mezreth answers questions put to him by researcher of Australia's true history Steven Strong. Steven asks a series of profound questions of Mezreth from philosophical, metaphysical, religious, to anthropology, archelogy, science and extra-terrestrial. Questioning the prevailing knowledge and seeking the truth about human history and civilizations such as Atlantis and Lemuria. Steven makes it clear that the information Lea shares from Mezreth is not channelling but a two-way conversation with this intelligence.

The breath of subject's information and complexity of the dialogue alone make it an absorbing, intriguing and fascinating must read."

Mary Rodwell, Founder and Principal of The Australian Close Encounter Resource Network www.acern.com.au

*OUT OF AUSTRALIA BY STEVEN & EVAN STRONG

In their startling new book, Steven and Evan Strong challenge the "out-of-Africa" theory. Based on fresh examination of both the DNA and archeological evidence, they conclude that modern humans originated from Australia, not Africa.

The original Australians (referred to by some as Aborigines), like so many indigenous peoples, are portrayed as "backward" and "primitive." Yet, as the Strongs demonstrate, original Australians had a rich culture, which may have sown the first seeds of spirituality in the world. They had the technology to make international seafaring voyages and have left traces in the Americas and possibly Japan, Southern India, Egypt, and elsewhere. They practiced brain surgery, invented the first hand tools, and had knowledge of penicillin.

This book brings together 30 years of intensive research in consultation with elders in the original Australian community. Among their conclusions are the following:

- There is evidence that humans existed in Australia 40,000 years before they existed in Australia.
- There were migrations of original Australians in large boats throughout the Indian/Pacific rim.
- Three distinct kinds of Homo sapiens are found in Australia.
- There is evidence from the Americas that debunks the out-of-Africa theory.
- The spiritual influence of the Aborigines is reflected in the religions of the world.

Through Amazon USA:
https://www.amazon.com/Out-Australia-Aborigines-Dreamtime-Human/dp/1571747818

Through Amazon AUSTRALIA:
https://www.amazon.com.au/Out-Australia-Aborigines-Dreamtime-Humandp/1571747818

Through Publisher:

https://redwheelweiser.com/book/out-of-australia-9781571747815/

"Could rewrite world history." --**Graham Hancock**

"No longer is the theory of creation out of Africa. It's here in Australia with the Originals." --**Michael Tellinger**

*BETWEEN A ROCK AND A HARD PLACE BY STEVEN & EVAN STRONG

It has often been said that humanity's history is a fabrication, littered with lies and omissions, but this has never been conclusively proven, until now. What has been recently found in Australia is unequivocal in rewriting convenient versions of ancient history and the genesis of modern humans.

We can now verify that Original Elders and Custodians of the Old Way are correct in insisting that Australia is the cradle of humanity, and "that all peoples of the world come from us." But it doesn't end there. Religion, art, burial, sailing, astronomy, navigation, democracy, gender equality and all the nobler hallmarks of civilised behaviour, are Original blessings exported from Australia.

There is ample archaeological evidence of the highest pedigree of an ancient sophisticated technology operating in Australia that is still unequalled by today's standards. And in seeking out the inspiration behind an Australian genesis of modern humans and the rise and fall of some very sophisticated technology, the Original Dreaming Stories and Keepers of the Old Ways stand united behind one non-Earthly standard bearer: the Pleiades.

Between a Rock and a Hard Place focuses on one incredibly profound site and a collection of sacred marked rocks. In combination, this archaeology redefines our collective past and repositions Homo sapiens sapiens ancestry, reminding us that the time is upon us to stop behaving like global vandals and realise that we are indeed, galactic citizens.

Through Amazon:
https://www.amazon.com/Between-Rock-Hard-Place-Australia/dp/0994526806

Through Authors Paperback (Signed) for Australian Customers:
https://forgottenorigin.com/shop

"I thoroughly enjoyed reading this manuscript and I feel so proud that I am a part of the Aboriginal people in our country...." **Associate Professor Rosemary Van Den Berg**

"They expose secrets that have long been suppressed regarding this mysterious indigenous nation and bring forward a controversial, yet thrilling new look at the progression of civilization on the Earth." **Dr Rita Louise**

"Wow what an amazing testimony. Such an absorbing blend of historical, geological and archaeological evidence supported by Original spirituality and knowledge!" **Belinda Rich (BA Archaeology/ Palaeoanthropology & MA History)**

* FORGOTTEN ORIGIN BY STEVEN & EVAN STRONG

Forgotten Origin is the third in a series of books dedicated to the first Homo sapiens: the Australian Aboriginal people. Steven Strong and Evan Strong continue in their investigation into the global impact of Aboriginal people sailing from, never to, Australia no less than 50,000 years ago, paying particular attention to the shared principles found within many Gnostic scriptures and the Dreaming. As radical as this theory may appear, the rigor applied, whether through mtDNA, Y Chromosomes, skull morphology or historical accounts, and the religious ancestry upon which this hidden history is founded, demands serious consideration. This is not their story. Steven Strong and Evan Strong make no claim to speak on behalf of anyone. They do, however, have the right to relay that which Aboriginal culture-custodians insist is true. The First Australians are unique, and in no way descended from Africans or any other race. Forgotten Origin is merely another reminder of this hidden truth.

Through Amazon:
https://www.amazon.com/Forgotten-Origin-Steven-Strong/dp/0761853340/

Book & eBook also available through University Press of America (Publisher):
https://rowman.com/ISBN/9780761853343

"Tremendous to see these issues being opened up - it is extremely stimulating to hear about these ideas …" -- **Howie Firth, patron of the International Festival of Philosophy, Science, and Theology**

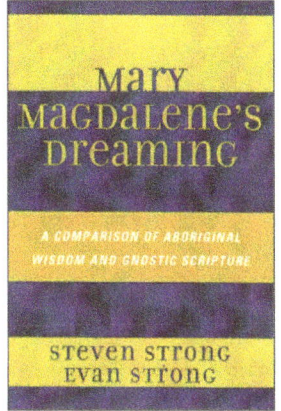

* MARY MAGDALENE'S DREAMING: A COMPARISON OF ABORIGINAL WISDOM AND GNOSTIC SCRIPTURES BY STEVEN & EVAN STRONG

In Mary Magdalene's Dreaming Steven Strong and Evan Strong continue their esoteric journey tracing the origins of religion that they began their first book, Constructing A New World Map. Strong and Strong examine the Gnostic Scriptures detailing the words and deeds of Mary and Jesus recently found at Nag Hammadi. They were, as Jesus stated in the Gospel of Thomas, custodians of a secret tradition. Jesus insisted he is but the caretaker of a "bubbling spring that I have tended". The authors further assert their belief that this "bubbling spring" is identical to the "secret place" aboriginal elder, Bill Neidjie, urges all to discover and it is their contention that a closer inspection of the ancient mystical spring Jesus and Mary accessed is evident in many Gnostic texts. The secret knowledge Mary and Jesus preached, stripped of cultural and geographic differences, is undoubtedly the purest replication of the Dreaming since the first mariners were banished from Australia.

Through Amazon:
http://www.amazon.com/Mary-Magdalenes-Dreaming-Comparison-Aboriginal/dp/0761842802/

Also available through University Press of America (Publisher):
https://rowman.com/ISBN/9780761842804

Associated with this Aboriginal time-line, is another recurring theme found throughout this book, which is extended in far greater depth in their second book ("Mary Magdalene's Dreaming"): the Aboriginal religious gnosis, called the Dreaming, was the primal philosophy that inspired a variety of religions, most particularly, the Isaic religion and Gnostic Christianity." **John McGrath retired Senior Lecturer (Newcastle University)**

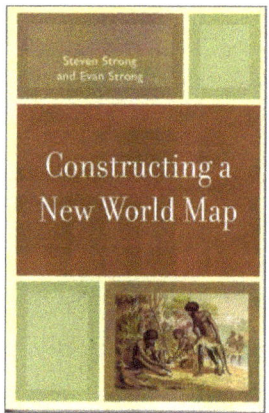

* CONSTRUCTING A NEW WORLD MAP BY STEVEN & EVAN STRONG

The first book in the trilogy. Nearly 50,000 years ago Australian Aboriginals set sail seeking new horizons. As they arrived on distant shores, they brought with them beliefs and a lifestyle unknown elsewhere. Their legacy was a mixed blessing. Although founding the basis of modern culture and cooperative living, they also exported knowledge of one errant practice.

These mariners did not volunteer to leave Australia, they were banished for selecting an agricultural practice that offended the Ancestral Spirits and the land. Living in the first Garden of Eden, as it was with Cain and Abel who chose to farm the land and animals, they were exiled for breaking a sacred covenant with the Dreaming. Common sense would dismiss these radical claims, but findings made at Aboriginal sites, ancient graves, and cave walls, along with new advances in genetics, have created circumstances that require the construction of a new world map.

Recent discovery of Gnostic texts at Nag Hammadi, particularly scriptures devoted to Mary and Jesus, reveal the ancient mystical tradition that began in the Dreaming was the inspiration behind their teachings. The message, preached by both the Dreaming, and Mary and Jesus is as relevant and important today as it was 50,000 years ago.

Through Amazon:
https://www.amazon.com/Constructing-New-World-Steven-Strongdp/0761840818/

Also available through University Press of America (Publisher):
https://rowman.com/ISBN/9780761840817

"I believe "Constructing a New World Map" is essential reading for any person with an interest in pre-history or Aboriginal culture ... I believe "Constructing a New World Map" is appropriately named and an essential read ... As controversial as this theory may first appear, it is based in solid facts, genes and mythology, and needs to be given credit and will generate a great deal of discussion." **John McGrath retired Senior Lecturer (Newcastle University)**

About the Authors:

Steven Strong: is a secondary school teacher with a background in Archaeology and Education. He was involved in the formation of a Graduate Diploma of Aboriginal Education for the N.S.W. Department of Education, writing units on Traditional Law and Contemporary History. He also co-authored the highly successful "Aboriginal Australia: A Language and Cultural kit".

Evan Strong: has a background in Anthropology & Indigenous Cultural Studies, Counselling & Mediation with a Bachelor's Degree in Social Sciences and Graduate Studies in Psychology. Evan has worked as a researcher for the Northern Rivers Area Health Service, a Social Worker, Teachers Aide, and a Funeral Director.

Figure 55: Evan & Steven Strong[1] (Evan - left & Steven – right)

They have spent many years learning, living and/or working with the Bundjalung Language Confederation (Northern Rivers Region of New South Wales), Ramindjeri (South Australia) and Gumilaroi peoples (Northern New South Wales). They operate under the doctrine of Wirritjin (Black Fella, White Fella Dreaming): In remembrance of Karno W...., spokesperson for the Ramindjeri. They work with a diverse informal network of Independent Researchers, Original Custodians/Elders, Patrons/Supporters and Friends.

Steven and Evan Strong are based near Byron Bay in Northern NSW.

Frederic Slater: (c1880- 10th March 1947) was a prolific Australian journalist, poet, researcher and folk-lore expert and President of the Australian Archaeological and Education Research Society.

Bibliography:

99designs, Deselect. Figure 51: Blue Kachina Star Prophecy. 2018. Picture. https://pixabay.com/photos/wallpaper-space-desktop-universe-3584226/.

Beve S., Aunty. Personal Communication, 2012.

Beve S., Aunty, and Gavi Duncan. Personal Communication, n.d.

Bower, Erik. Figure 1: Frederic Slater's Grave Marker. 2015. Photograph.

———. Figure 34: Mount Yengo. 2016. Photograph.

Bowler, James Maurice. Figure 42: Mungo Man. Unknown. Photograph. sent by James Maurice Bowler. https://commons.wikimedia.org/wiki/File:Mungo_Man.jpg.

Budai, Ildi. Figure 28: Hieroglyphs at Bambara/Kariong. 2016. Photograph.

Cardinal Moran, Patrick F. Figure 18: Discovery of Australia by de Quiros in the Year 1606. 2006. Cover Page. http://www.gutenberg.net.au/ebooks06/0600641h.html.

Claire, Taylor. Figure 36: The Wandjina. July 21, 2007. Photograph. Wandjina Rock Art. https://commons.wikimedia.org/wiki/File:Wandjina_rock_art.jpg.

Curnoe, Darren. Figure 41: WLH 50 Skullcap. January 20, 2011. https://doi.org/10.4061/2011/632484. https://commons.wikimedia.org/wiki/File:Willandra_Lakes_Human_50_calvaria.png.

Darkmoon_Art, Dorothe. Figure 12: To Hand Over. 2018. https://pixabay.com/photos/world-earth-globe-keep-give-take-3258865/.

Evans, Eamon. Whatever Happened to Ned Kelly's Head. 1st ed. South Melbourne, Victoria: Affirm Press, 2020.

Flood, Josephine. Archaeology of the Dreamtime: The Story of Prehistoric Australia and Its People. Marleston, South Australia: JB Publishing, n.d.

Fox, David. Figure 21: Atlantis, Underwater, Ruins, Temple. 2020. Picture. https://pixabay.com/photos/underwater-ruins-temple-water-5151969/.

Frankzed. Figure 5: Brown Hawk. April 13, 2012. Brown Falcon Uploaded by snowmanradio. https://commons.wikimedia.org/wiki/File:Falco_berigora_-Phillip_Island,_Victoria,_Australia_-flying-8.jpg.

Fullagar, Richard, David Price, and Lesley Head. "Early Human Occupation of Northern Australia: Archaeology and Thermoluminescence Dating of Jinmium Rock Shelter, Northern Territory." Top 100 Citations 70 (December 1, 1996): 751–73. https://doi.org/10.1017/S0003598X00084040.

Goddard, R. H., and Frederic Slater. "Burragurru or Devil's Rock: An Aboriginal Burial Ground in the Wollombi District [Manuscript]. - Trove," 1937. https://trove.nla.gov.au/work/35581115.

———. Figure 9: Cover Page of Goddard & Slater's Paper (with Cancelled Stamp) - Burragurru or Devil's Rock : An Aboriginal Burial Ground in the Wollombi District. 1937. Cover.

———. Figure 19: Cover Page of Goddard & Slater's Paper- Burragurru or Devil's Rock : An Aboriginal Burial Ground in the Wollombi District. 1937. Cover Page, Cancelled Stamps & Close-ups.

———. Figure 20: Tropical Medicine and Public Health Cancelled Stamp Goddard & Slater's Paper- Burragurru or Devil's Rock : An Aboriginal Burial Ground in the Wollombi District. 1937. Cancelled Stamps.

———. Figure 23: Burragurru or Devil's Rock: An Aboriginal Burial Ground in the Wollombi District. 1937. https://trove.nla.gov.au/work/35581115.

Gresley, Alan, and Gavin Bragg. Figure 29: The Shaft. 2013 2012. Photograph - College.

Gunson, Niel. "Dunlop, Eliza Hamilton (1796–1880)." In Australian Dictionary of Biography, Vol. 1. Canberra: National Centre of Biography, Australian National University, 1966. https://adb.anu.edu.au/biography/dunlop-eliza-hamilton-2007.

Jarmbi'je. Personal Communication, 2014.

Kapiteli, Lea. Back Cover. 2023. Mixed Media.

Klaatsch, Professor / M.D. Hermann. Figure 44: Professor / M.D. Hermann Klaatsch. 1923. Photograph.

———. The Evolution and Progress of Mankind. Edited by Profosser / M.D. Adolf Heilborn. Translated by Joseph McCabe. New York, NY: Frederick A. Stokes Company Publishers, 1923.

Lawlor, Robert. Voices of the First Day: Awakening in the Aboriginal Dreamtime. Rochester, Vermont: Inner Traditions International, 1991.

López Polanco, Andrés. Figure 14: Philip III of Spain. circa 1617. Painting. https://en.wikipedia.org/w/index.php?title=Philip_III_of_Spain&oldid=1120225496.

Mail, The. "Came From Africa To Australia." Mail (Adelaide, SA : 1912 - 1954). October 23, 1937.

———. Figure 13: Murree Gwalda- From (Came From Africa To Australia). October 23, 1937. Newspaper Article. http://nla.gov.au/nla.news-article55070946.

MDRX. Figure 38: Lake George. August 6, 2015. Photograph. Own work. https://commons.wikimedia.org/wiki/File:Lake_George,_New_South_Wales.JPG.

Montfaucon, Bernard de. Figure 35: Yaldabaoth - Montfaucon's L'antiquité Expliquée et Représentée En Figures (Found on Gnostic Gem). 1722. https://en.wikipedia.org/w/index.php?title=Yaldabaoth&oldid=1122856658.

Moran, Patrick F. Cardinal. "Discovery of Australia by de Quiros in the Year 1606." A Project Gutenberg of Australia & The Australian Catholic Truth Society, 2006. https://gutenberg.net.au/ebooks06/0600641h.html.

Morning Herald, The Sydney. "The Bone Keeper's Dilemma." The Sydney Morning Herald, June 9, 2003. https://www.smh.com.au/world/the-bone-keepers-dilemma-20030609-gdgwg2.html.

National Parks & Wildlife Service. Figure 27: Rock Engraving Durramullan. Unknown. Photograph from Pamphlet.

Newcastle Sun. "Presented to Frederic Slater ... (Award)." Newcastle Sun, March 29, 1924.

Nuñez, Biblioteca Rector Machado y. Figure 16: Pedro Fernández de Quirós. November 15, 2019. Picture. https://www.flickr.com/photos/37667416@N04/49789104452/. https://commons.wikimedia.org/wiki/File:A055a161_0584.jpg.

Olley, Olivia, and Brett Waller. Figure 6: Karno W. 2016. Photograph & Text.

Pixell, Smiling. Figure 48: Great Record Book. 2016. Picture. https://pixabay.com/photos/hand-fire-rosetta-stone-fingers-1393606/.

Publishers Pty Ltd, Macquarie Dictionary. Macquarie Encyclopedic Dictionary: Signature Edition. 2nd ed. Sydney, Australia: Australia's Heritage Publishing Pty Ltd, 2011.

Riddhi, Raymond Johnson, and Edith May Rumbel. Figure 26: God of Inheritance (Rock Engraving & Glyph Comparison). 1997 2011. Photograph & Glyph Diagram.

Rueparadis. Figure 40: Lake Mungo. June 21, 2018. Photograph. Own work. https://commons.wikimedia.org/wiki/File:Lake_Mungo_lunette.jpg.

Schmerbeck, Erica. Figure 3: Book Cover of "Between a Rock and Hard Place", by Steven & Evan Strong. 2016. Book Cover.

Scribe, Hunefer. Figure 22: The Ancient Egyptian Book of the Dead Depicts a Scene in Which a Deceased Person's Heart Is Weighed against the Feather of Truth (Papyrus of Hunefer). Papyrus, height: 39.8 cm (15.6 in) ; width: 550 cm (18 ft) dimensions QS:P2048,+39.8U174728 dimensions QS:P2049,+550U174728. British Museum. Accessed November 29, 2022. https://commons.wikimedia.org/wiki/File:El_pesado_del_coraz%C3%B3n_en_el_Papiro_de_Hunefer.jpg.

Slater, Frederic. "ABORIGINAL ROCK CARVINGS." Sydney Morning Herald (NSW: 1842 - 1954). January 23, 1937.

———. Figure 2: Cover of Slater's Scribes of the Stone Age. 1937. Cover.

———. "Gladstone and Its Harbour." Mudgee Guardian. 1899.

———. Scribes of the Stone Age, 1937.

Slater, Frederic, and Richard Patterson, ed. Personal Letters - Correspondences - Notes. 2013th ed. No. 1-19 & Original 53-61. Archaeological and Education Research Society, 1939.

Socha, Arek. Figure 11: Key. 2017. Photograph. https://pixabay.com/illustrations/key-keyhole-lock-security-unlock-2114046/.

Somma, Ryan. Figure 43: Kow Swamp 1. January 1, 1980. Photograph. Homo Sapiens

13,000 to 9,000 Years Old. https://commons.wikimedia.org/wiki/File:Kow_Swamp1-Homo_sapiens.jpg.

Soon, Heung. Figure 54: Book of Translations - More to Follow. 2019. Photograph. https://pixabay.com/photos/note-diary-phrases-record-book-4121949/.

Stringer, Chris. "A Metrical Study of WLH-50 Calvaria." Journal of Human Evolution 34 (1998): 327–32.

Strong, Dellene. Figure 25: Daramulum's Head and Ngalbal Represented in Emu Form with Her Shield. 2023. Diagram.

———. Figure 46: Southern Law Confederation Map. 2023. Diagram.

Strong, Dellene, and Lea Kapiteli. Front Cover. 2023. Mixed Media - Drawing.

Strong, Evan. Figure 4: Standing Stones Site. 2013. Photograph.

———. Figure 8: Burragurra. 2014. Photograph.

———. Figure 32: Bulgandry. 2012. Photograph.

———. Figure 37: Eleven Sites with Anomalous Dates. 2015. Table.

———. Figure 39: Replica of Panaramitee Crocodile Engraving. 2015. Photograph.

———. Figure 51: Frederic Slater's Award. 2023. Photograph.

———. Figure 52: Frederic Slater's Award. 2023. Photograph.

———. Figure 53: Close-up of Frederic Slater's Award. 2023. Photograph.

Strong, Steven. Figure 33: Diagram of Bulgandry (Belt of Orion). 2012. Diagram.

Strong, Steven, Karno W., and Frederic Slater. Figure 45: Possum Dreaming - Mix of Karno's & Slater's Symbols. 2013, 1939 2015. Diagram.

Taken. Figure 49: Nemo. 2014. Photograph. https://pixabay.com/photos/clownfish-anemonefish-fish-sea-426567/.

Todoavante. Figure 17: Luís Vaz de Torres. 2011. Picture. https://todoavante.es/index.php?title=Archivo:LuiVaeTorr1.JPG.

Unknown. Figure 7: Frederic Slater - The Wrong Person/Photograph - Hoax or Key to Solving Ancient Mystery? (The West Australian Via The Courier Mail). March 19, 2017. Photograph. https://thewest.com.au/news/qld/is-australias-stonehenge-near-mullumbimby-where-civilisation-began-or-historical-hoax-ng-8a0fe799bf3e97d69deb9eb744a36169.

Unknown, Author. Figure 10: Eliza Hamilton Dunlop. c.1820s. Frontspiece Illustration.

———. Figure 15: Francis Moran (Cardinal). circa 1900. Photograph. https://en.wikipedia.org/w/index.php?title=Francis_Moran_(cardinal)&oldid=1109104761.

———. Figure 47: R. H. Mathews. 1909. Photograph. [1]. https://commons.wikimedia.org/wiki/File:R_H_Mathews.jpg.

———. Figure 50: Rosetta Stone. 2009. Picture. https://commons.wikimedia.org/wiki/File:Rosetta_Stone_BW.jpeg.

W., Karno. More DNA, 2014.

———. Personal Communication, 2014.

———. Sothern Law Confederation, 2014.

Wood, Samarah. Figure 30: Bone Artefact. 2014. Photograph.

———. Figure 31: Metal Artefact. 2014. Photograph.

———. Figure 55: Evan & Steven Strong. 2016. Photograph.

Wyatt, Jon. "Article," August 13, 2022.

———. "Frederic Slater," July 6, 2022.

———. "Frederic Slater," July 11, 2022.

———. "Frederic Worral Slater," July 22, 2022.

Yanna Muru, Evan. Figure 24: Ankh Engraving with Ibis Footprint. 2010. Photograph.

Endnotes:
REFERENCES & NOTES:

- **Within this References & Notes section:** the specific term/concept/word being defined is in **Bold**
- The word **Aboriginal** is replaced with the word **Original** to describe the Indigenous Peoples of Australia.
- Surnames of deceased Australia Original Elders, Custodians and peoples are with-held to observe protocols of respect and culture.
- Other names have been changed to ensure the security and safety of some of our sources.

Front Matter

Front Cover: Dellene Strong and Erica Schmerbeck, Front Cover, 2023, Mixed Media - Drawing, 2023. Dallas Nock, Photography

Back Cover: Erica Schmerbeck, Back Cover, 2023, Mixed Media, 2023. Dallas Nock, Photography

1 Erik Bower, Figure 1: Frederic Slater's Grave Marker, 2015, Photograph, 2015

Introduction:

1 **Frederic Slater:** (c1880- 10th March 1947) was a prolific Australian journalist, poet, researcher and folk-lore expert and President of the Australian Archaeological and Education Research Society.

2 Frederic Slater, Scribes of the Stone Age, 1937.

3 **Sky Heroes:** Creation Spirits who descended from the sky above. They were instrumental in the creation of humanity in Australia.

4 **Original:** The word Aboriginal is replaced with the word Original to describe the Indigenous Peoples of Australia.

5 Frederic Slater, Figure 2: Cover of Slater's Scribes of the Stone Age, 1937, Cover, 1937.

Chapter 1: Hidden and Lost in a Forgotten Filing Cabinet

1 Frederic Slater and Richard Patterson, ed., Personal Letters - Correspondences - Notes, 2013th ed., No. 1-19 & Original 53-61 (Archaeological and Education Research Society, 1939).

2 **Ramindjeri:** Australian Original Tribe and Lands incorporating Karta (Kangaroo Island), Victor Harbour Encounter Bay area, to Adelaide and River Torrens within South Australia.

3 Erica Schmerbeck, Figure 3: Book Cover of "Between a Rock and Hard Place", by Steven & Evan Strong, 2016, Book Cover, 2016.
4 Evan Strong, Figure 4: Standing Stones Site, 2013, Photograph, 2013.
5 Jarmbi'je, Personal Communication, 2014.
6 Frankzed, Figure 5: Brown Hawk, April 13, 2012, April 13, 2012, Brown Falcon Uploaded by snowmanradio, https://commons.wikimedia.org/wiki/File:Falco_berigora_-Phillip_Island,_Victoria,_Australia_-flying-8.jpg (Rights: Creative Commons Attribution 2.0 Generic.).
7 Karno W., Personal Communication, 2014.
8 Olivia Olley and Brett Waller, Figure 6: Karno W., 2016, Photograph & Text, 2016 (Special Thanks to Christine Walker & The Ramindjeri for permission to use this picture).

Chapter 2: Frederic Slater: A Genius or Mischievous?

1 **Professor A. P. Elkin:** Elkin wrote Aboriginal Men of High Degree, where he acknowledged that Clever-fellas have many supernatural powers. He was the first professor of Anthropology at Sydney University.

2 Unknown, Figure 7: Frederic Slater - The Wrong Person/Photograph - Hoax or Key to Solving Ancient Mystery? (The West Australian Via The Courier Mail), March 19, 2017, Photograph, March 19, 2017, https://thewest.com.au/news/qld/is-australias-stonehenge-near-mullumbimby-where-civilisation-began-or-historical-hoax-ng-8a0fe799bf3e97d69deb9eb744a36169.
3 Frederic Slater, "ABORIGINAL ROCK CARVINGS.," Sydney Morning Herald (NSW: 1842 - 1954), January 23, 1937, 14.
4 The Mail, "Came From Africa To Australia," Mail (Adelaide, SA : 1912 - 1954), October 23, 1937, 6.
5 Evan Strong, Figure 8: Burragurra, 2014, Photograph, 2014.
6 Slater, "ABORIGINAL ROCK CARVINGS.," 14.

7 **Wollombi:** is a village in the Hunter Valley Region of N.S.W. (New South Wales) just north of Sydney, in Australia.

8 R. H. Goddard and Frederic Slater, "Burragurru or Devil's Rock: An Aboriginal Burial Ground in the Wollombi District [Manuscript]. - Trove," 1937, Cover Page, https://trove.nla.gov.au/work/35581115.
9 Slater, "ABORIGINAL ROCK CARVINGS.," Cover Page.
10 R. H. Goddard and Frederic Slater, Figure 9: Cover Page of Goddard & Slater's Paper (with Cancelled Stamp) - Burragurru or Devil's Rock : An Aboriginal Burial Ground in the Wollombi District, 1937, Cover, 1937.

11 **Eliza Hamilton Dunlop:** (1796 -1880) ethnographer of Australian Original folklore, language, poetry and songs. Also, a respected poet /lyric writer and an Australian Original welfare activist. See: Niel Gunson, "Dunlop, Eliza Hamilton (1796–1880)," in Australian Dictionary of Biography, vol. 1 (Canberra: National Centre of Biography, Australian National University, 1966), https://adb.anu.edu.au/biography/dunlop-eliza-hamilton-2007.

12 **Roy Goddard:** Archaeologist, colleague of Frederic Slater and grandson of Eliza Dunlop.

13 Author Unknown, Figure 10: Eliza Hamilton Dunlop, c.1820s, Frontspiece Illustration, c.1820s.
14 Slater, Scribes of the Stone Age, 3 (Chapter 1: Pharaohs of the South Land).
15 Slater, 3.
16 Slater, 4.
17 Slater, 29 (Chapter 3: Symbolic Writing).
18 Slater, 4 (Chapter 1: Pharaohs of the South Land).
19 Slater, 11.
20 Slater, 12.
21 Slater, 4-5.
22 Arek Socha, Figure 11: Key, 2017, Photograph, 2017, https://pixabay.com/illustration key-keyhole-lock-security-unlock-2114046/ (Rights: Pixabay License).
23 Slater, Scribes of the Stone Age, 2.
24 Slater, 8.
25 Slater, 9.
26 Slater, 5.
27 Slater, 29 (Chapter 3: Symbolic Writing).
28 Slater, 4 (Chapter 1: Pharaohs of the South Land).
29 Slater, 4.
30 Slater, 6.
31 Dorothe Darkmoon_Art, Figure 12: To Hand Over, 2018, 2018, https://pixabay.com/photos/world-earth-globe-keep-give-take-3258865/ (Rights: Pixabay License).

Chapter 3: The Inconvenient Truths

1 Eamon Evans, Whatever Happened to Ned Kelly's Head, 1st ed. (South Melbourne, Victoria: Affirm Press, 2020), 235.
2 Evans, 235.
3 Evans, 235.
4 Evans, 235.
5 Evans, 235.
6 Evans, 235.
7 Evans, 235.
8 Evans, 235.
9 Evans, 235.
10 Evans, 235.
11 Frederic Slater, "Gladstone and Its Harbour," Mudgee Guardian, 1899 Anon.
12 Jon Wyatt, "Frederic Slater," July 11, 2022.
13 Jon Wyatt, "Frederic Worral Slater," July 22, 2022.
14 Goddard and Slater, "Burragurru or Devil's Rock: An Aboriginal Burial Ground in the Wollombi District [Manuscript]. - Trove."
15 Slater, "ABORIGINAL ROCK CARVINGS.," 14.
16 The Mail, Figure 13: Murree Gwalda- From (Came From Africa To Australia), October 23, 1937, Newspaper Article, October 23, 1937, http://nla.gov.au/nla.news-article55070946.

17 **Patrick Francis Cardinal Moran:** (16th Sept.- !6th Aug. 1911) Born in Ireland and

3rd Catholic Archbishop of Sydney and 1st cardinal from Australia. An intellectual with a Doctorate, spoke 5 languages, edited Irish ecclesiastical historical documents and a professor of scripture. 250,000 people attended his funeral procession.

18 **Philip III of Spain:** (14 April 1578 – 31 March 1621) was King of Spain (also King Philip II of Portugal, Naples, Sicily and Duke of Milan {1598-1621}), and of the House of Habsburg.

19 Andrés López Polanco, Figure 14: Philip III of Spain, circa 1617, Painting, circa 1617, https://en.wikipedia.org/w/index.php?title=Philip_III_of_Spain&oldid=1120225496 (Rights: Creative Commons Attribution-ShareAlike License).
20 Wyatt, "Frederic Slater," July 11, 2022.
21 Wyatt.
22 Author Unknown, Figure 15: Francis Moran (Cardinal), circa 1900, Photograph, circa 1900, https://en.wikipedia.org/w/index.php?title=Francis_Moran_(cardinal)&oldid=1109104761 (Rights: Creative Commons Attribution-ShareAlike License).

23 **Pedro Fernández de Quirós:** (1563-1614) a Portuguese navigator under Spanish service, involved with the Spanish exploration of the Pacific Ocean, notably a 1605-1606 journey in search for Australia, also involved with explorations to the Philippines, Cook Islands, Kiribati, Vanuatu, and the Solomon Islands. Founded a new order of Chivalry- Knights of the Holy Ghost.

24 Biblioteca Rector Machado y Nuñez, Figure 16: Pedro Fernández de Quirós, November 15, 2019, Picture, November 15, 2019, https://www.flickr.com/photos/37667416@N04/49789104452/, https://commons.wikimedia.org/wiki/File:A055a161_0584.jpg (Rights: Public Domain).
25 Jon Wyatt, "Frederic Slater," July 6, 2022.
26 Wyatt.

27 **Luís Vaz de Torres:** A Galician (North-Western Spain) Captain and Explorer in the 16th and 17th Centuries, notable for the navigation of the Torres Strait (the strait that separates Australia and Papua New Guinea). Second-in-command in Pedro Fernandes de Queiró's search for Australia.

28 Todoavante, Figure 17: Luís Vaz de Torres, 2011, Picture, 2011, https://todoavante.es/index.php?title=Archivo:LuiVaeTorr1.JPG.
29 Patrick F. Cardinal Moran, Figure 18: Discovery of Australia by de Quiros in the Year 1606, 2006, Cover Page, 2006, http://www.gutenberg.net.au/ebooks06/0600641h.html (Rights: Project Gutenberg of Australia License).
30 Goddard and Slater, "Burragurru or Devil's Rock: An Aboriginal Burial Ground in the Wollombi District [Manuscript]. - Trove," Cover Page.
31 R. H. Goddard and Frederic Slater, Figure 19: Cover Page of Goddard & Slater's Paper- Burragurru or Devil's Rock : An Aboriginal Burial Ground in the Wollombi District, 1937, Cover Page, Cancelled Stamps & Close-ups, 1937.
32 Goddard and Slater, "Burragurru or Devil's Rock: An Aboriginal Burial Ground in the Wollombi District [Manuscript]. - Trove," Cover Page.
33 R. H. Goddard and Frederic Slater, Figure 20: Tropical Medicine and Public Health Cancelled Stamp Goddard & Slater's Paper- Burragurru or Devil's Rock : An Aboriginal Burial Ground in the Wollombi District, 1937, Cancelled Stamps, 1937, 2.

Chapter 4: "The Pharaohs of the South Land"

1 Slater, Scribes of the Stone Age, 1–15.

Chapter 5: Civilised Behaviour

1 Slater, 1.
2 Slater, 2.
3 Slater, 2.
4 Slater, 2–3.
5 Slater, 3.
6 Slater, 3.

7 **Carbon 14:** Atmospheric carbon is usually found as one of two isotopes: Carbon 12 and Carbon 14. Carbon 14 is an unstable isotope that decomposes into Carbon 12 over time. Carbon dating can be used to date organic substances that are less than 50,000 years old.

8 **OSL (Optically Stimulated Luminescence) ESR Uranium Cation Spectrometry:** A dating technique that involves assessing mineral grains that were exposed to sunlight and or heating notably the decay of radioactive material and the time taken to reach this state. Dateable age range is a few years ago to >1 million years ago.

9 **Thermoluminescence:** dating via the measurement of collective radiation dose of elapsed time crystalline minerals within a material that were heated or have had sunlight exposure. Thermoluminescence begins when the material to be analysed/measured is heated, a weaker light signal is emitted that is proportional to absorbed radiation of the material. Especially used in dating of sediments and ceramics.

10 **mtDNA:** DNA found in the Mitochondria (portion of cell which generated energy), Human mtDNA are clones passed on by the mother with little genetic difference from generation to generation. This type of DNA consists of 37 genes and 16,568 base pairs.

11 David Fox, Figure 21: Atlantis, Underwater, Ruins, Temple, 2020, Picture, 2020, https://pixabay.com/photos/underwater-ruins-temple-water-5151969/ (Rights: Pixabay License).
12 Slater, Scribes of the Stone Age, 6.
13 Slater, 15.
14 Slater, 14.
15 Slater, 11.
16 Slater, 11.
17 Slater, 11.
18 Slater, 5.
19 Slater, 5.
20 Slater, 5.
21 Slater, 5.

22 Slater, 5–6.
23 Slater, 4.

24 **Egyptian Book of the Dead:** (or the Book of Coming [or Going] Forth by Day). This book is an Egyptian funerary text, possibly as old as 1580-1350 B.C., it is usually illustrated. A collection of spells, charms, magic etc. to be used in the afterlife by the deceased to guide them through the tribulations involved in the underworld.

25 Slater, Scribes of the Stone Age, 3.
26 Hunefer Scribe, Figure 22: The Ancient Egyptian Book of the Dead Depicts a Scene in Which a Deceased Person's Heart Is Weighed against the Feather of Truth (Papyrus of Hunefer), papyrus, height: 39.8 cm (15.6 in) ; width: 550 cm (18 ft) dimensions QS:P2048,+39.8U174728 dimensions QS:P2049,+550U174728, British Museum, accessed November 29, 2022, https://commons.wikimedia.org/wiki/File:El_pesado_del_coraz%C3%B3n_en_el_Papiro_de_Hunefer.jpg (Rights: Public Domain).
27 Slater and Patterson, ed., Personal Letters - Correspondences - Notes, no. 6.
28 Slater, Scribes of the Stone Age, 4.
29 Macquarie Dictionary Publishers Pty Ltd, Macquarie Encyclopedic Dictionary: Signature Edition, 2nd ed. (Sydney, Australia: Australia's Heritage Publishing Pty Ltd, 2011),
30 Publishers Pty Ltd, 15.
31 Slater, Scribes of the Stone Age, 5.

Chapter 6: "Words on the Rocks"

1 Slater, 16–19 & 27–28.

Chapter 7: Wollombi and Gosford: Home Base

1 Slater, 16.
2 Slater, 16.
3 Slater, 16.
4 Slater, 17.
5 R. H. Goddard and Frederic Slater, Figure 23: Burragurru or Devil's Rock: An Aboriginal Burial Ground in the Wollombi District, 1937, 1937, 18, https://trove.nla.gov.au/work/35581115 Plate IV.

6 **Ankh:** widely used symbol, use in hieroglyphic texts, its origin is under debate, it may represent males and female reproductive parts, sun on the horizon with its path, and a girdle, has magical protective properties. Associated with the hieroglyph meaning life or breath life and often depicted with gods and goddesses.

7 **Thoth:** a prominent Ancient Egyptian god of importance, usually depicted as an Ibis headed man, sometimes as a baboon. It was the deity of the moon, wisdom, writing, science, magic, and judgment (all the good stuff). In the baboon guise is of equilibrium, in the underworld would weigh the deceased heart against a feather for judgment.

8   Evan Yanna Muru, Figure 24: Ankh Engraving with Ibis Footprint, 2010, Photograph, 2010.

9   **Daramulum (Darhumulan, Daramulan, Dhurramoolun or Dharramaalan):** a sky hero, Biaime's son, is a shapeshifter, whose voice can be heard through the bull-roarer and is associated with the Southern Cross (Alpha Crucis)

10   **Baiame (Biame/ Baiame / Bhaiame/ Baayami, Baayama or Byamee):** Sky Father/All Father came from the skies to create the lands, give laws and culture etc then returned to the skies. The creator Sky-Hero for many Original Nations of south-eastern NSW.

11   **Ngalbal:** (Emu in the Sky) the Emu-wife of Daramulum, a sky hero and is her head associated with the Southern Cross Constellation.

12   Dellene Strong, Figure 25: Daramulum's Head and Ngalbal Represented in Emu Form with Her Shield, 2023, Diagram, 2023.
13   Riddhi, Raymond Johnson, and Edith May Rumbel, Figure 26: God of Inheritance (Rock Engraving & Glyph Comparison), 1997 2011, Photograph & Glyph Diagram, 1997 2011, Glyph no. 539, 16 Photo by Riddhi 2011 & Glyph from "Basic Hieroglyphia"1997 (Edition Senff).
14   National Parks & Wildlife Service, Figure 27: Rock Engraving Durramullan, Unknown, Photograph from Pamphlet, Unknown Image Supplied by Angel John Gallard.
15   Ildi Budai, Figure 28: Hieroglyphs at Bambara/Kariong, 2016, Photograph, 2016.
16   Alan Gresley and Gavin Bragg, Figure 29: The Shaft, 2013 2012, Photograph - College, 2013 2012.
17   Samarah Wood, Figure 30: Bone Artefact, 2014, Photograph, 2014.
18   Samarah Wood, Figure 31: Metal Artefact, 2014, Photograph, 2014.
19   Aunty Beve S. and Gavi Duncan, Personal Communication, n.d.
20   Evan Strong, Figure 32: Bulgandry, 2012, Photograph, 2012.
21   Aunty Beve S., Personal Communication, 2012.
22   Beve S.
23   Steven Strong, Figure 33: Diagram of Bulgandry (Belt of Orion), 2012, Diagram, 2012.
24   Goddard and Slater, "Burragurru or Devil's Rock: An Aboriginal Burial Ground in the Wollombi District [Manuscript]. - Trove," 11.
25   Goddard and Slater, 11–12.
26   Erik Bower, Figure 34: Mount Yengo, 2016, Photograph, 2016.
27   Goddard and Slater, "Burragurru or Devil's Rock: An Aboriginal Burial Ground in the Wollombi District [Manuscript]. - Trove," 12.
28   Goddard and Slater, 12.
29   Goddard and Slater, 12.
30   Goddard and Slater, 11.
31   Goddard and Slater, 11.
32   Goddard and Slater, 13.

33   **Yaldabaoth, Jaldabaoth, Ildabaoth:** an evil/misguided/ignorant/incompetent deity and creator/Demiurge (artisan/creator/maintainer of physical universe) within Gnosticism. Often represented as a lion headed serpent. Keeps us (our souls) imprisoned in our bodies. Also is the son of Sophia (Wisdom) and was created imperfectly.

34   Bernard de Montfaucon, Figure 35: Yaldabaoth - Montfaucon's L'antiquité Expliquée et

Représentée En Figures (Found on Gnostic Gem), 1722, 1722, https://en.wikipedia.org/w/index.php?title=Yaldabaoth&oldid=1122856658 (Rights: Creative Commons Attribution-ShareAlike License).
35 Beve S., Personal Communication.

36 **Wandjina Wanjina, Wondjina, Gulingi:** Cloud/rain spirits from Original mythology, depicted in rock art in Western Australia (The Kimberley region – See ref. below). Distinctive appearance with no mouths, some parallels to Off-world Alien appearance have been suggested.

37 **The Kimberley:** a region (423,517km2/ 163,521 sq. miles) in the north of Western Australia, surrounded by the Indian Ocean in the west, the Timor Sea to the north, and the Great Sandy and Tanami Deserts to the south. The Region hosts Original Rock Art, and many well-known indigenous artists come from this region. It has a monsoonal climate with a rugged sandstone landscape.

38 Taylor Claire, Figure 36: The Wandjina, July 21, 2007, Photograph, July 21, 2007, Wandjina Rock Art, https://commons.wikimedia.org/wiki/File:Wandjina_rock_art.jpg (Rights: Creative Commons Attribution-Share Alike 2.0 Generic).
39 Goddard and Slater, "Burragurru or Devil's Rock: An Aboriginal Burial Ground in the Wollombi District [Manuscript]. - Trove," 11.
40 Goddard and Slater, 11.
41 Goddard and Slater, 11.
42 Goddard and Slater, 11.

Chapter 8: "Symbolic Writing"

1 Slater, Scribes of the Stone Age, 29–46.

Chapter 9: The Date Would be Nearer to 100,000 years

1 **Great Barrier Reef:** Jim Bowler and the Australian specialist in core extraction, Gurdup Singh, along with Peter Ouwendyke, co-wrote a paper in 1983 declaring their unanimous conclusion of the analysis of a core sample taken from the Great Barrier Reef. They were in agreement that the dramatic increase in charcoal in the core extracted from the reef was due to the fire-stick farming initiated by the Original people and that this began 186,000 years ago.

2 **Lake George:** An inland lake situated between Goulburn (N.S.W.) and Canberra (A.C.T.). It has a remarkable history of rapidly fluctuating lake levels. The lake can virtually disappear overnight; this fact has created many bizarre theories and intense speculation.

3 **Panaramitee:** engraving found at Panaramitee (South Australia) has attracted a lot of attention. It was discovered in 1929 and is an plan (aerial) view of a sea crocodile (Crocodylus porosus). Not only is it a fine piece of art, it was chiselled into rock over 75,000 years ago.

4 **Jinmium:** According to a challenging paper compiled by a highly respected group of scholars (Drs. Richard Fullagher, Lesley Head, and David Price), there is evidence of art via ochre use and pecking taking place sometime between 75,000 and 116,000 years ago at Jinmium (N.T.).

5 **Lake Mungo:** Part of a series of inland lakes that were once linked together to form the Willandra Lakes System, which created somewhere close to the reputed inland sea early explorers vainly sought. The entire system dried up around 15,000 years ago, and since then has remained in that state. Lake Mungo is the most prolific archaeological site yet discovered in Australia with extensive evidence of human remains and by-products.

6 **Kow Swamp:** Found in Victoria, it is the site of the largest human burial site of prehistoric times. Contains only robust (see below*) skeletons and added considerable weight to the belief they were a separate species of sapiens. A freshwater lake currently and formally a swamp, located in the Mallee region of north-central Victoria.
*__Robust:__ A more archaic-featured hominid with thicker bones, continuous eyebrow ridge and a receding forehead. However, their intellect was at least the equal of the gracile species. These hominids were part of the Homo sapiens sapiens family and should not be confused or categorised with Homo erectus (See below#). This strand is a modern human; aware of the Creator, carrying out their own unique funerary rites and living a lifestyle that was almost the same as their gracile (see below^) 'cousins'.
Homo erectus: An extinct species of hominid that immediately preceded Homo sapiens. Homo erectus is claimed to have first appeared about 2 million years ago, and was a hunter-gather, made tools and fires.
^**Gracile:** A fine-featured Homo sapiens sapiens; the physiology and intellect is identical to modern people. Such a person could literally walk through the streets today unnoticed.

7 **Cossack:** The last robust site (Western Australia) discovered (6,500 years B.P.). The most interesting aspect about this skull is that it has the steepest angle receding from the eyebrow ridge of any robust skull yet detected.

8 Evan Strong, Figure 37: Eleven Sites with Anomalous Dates, 2015, Table, 2015.

9 **Professor Jim Bowler:** a geologist and geo-morphologist (Australian National University and now University of Melbourne).

10 **Dr Gurdup/Gurdip Singh:** from A.N.U. (Australian National University) he was the first scholar to present evidence that indicated Aboriginal presence at Lake George around 120,000 years ago.

11 **Great Barrier Reef:** the world's largest coral reef system with 900 islands, 2,900 reefs, and an area of 344,000 km2 and a length of 2,300 km. Its location is off the Queensland coast in the Coral sea and is one of the seven natural wonders of the world.

12 **Emeritus Professor Richard Wright:** archaeologist/anthropologist with specialisation in Australian prehistory especially stone tools and osteology (bones).

13 MDRX, Figure 38: Lake George, August 6, 2015, Photograph, August 6, 2015, Own work, https://commons.wikimedia.org/wiki/File:Lake_George,_New_South_Wales.JPG

(Rights: Creative Commons Attribution-Share Alike 4.0 International).

14 **Dr Josephine Flood:** archaeologist, author, lecturer from A.N.U., award winner and Australia Heritage Commission Assistant Director from 1979-91. Her book "Archaeology of the Dreamtime" is a bestselling book on archaeology.

15 Josephine Flood, Archaeology of the Dreamtime: The Story of Prehistoric Australia and Its People (Marleston, South Australia: JB Publishing, n.d.), 180.
16 Flood, 180.
17 Flood, 180.
18 Flood, 180.
19 Evan Strong, Figure 39: Replica of Panaramitee Crocodile Engraving, 2015, Photograph, 2015.
20 Flood, Archaeology of the Dreamtime: The Story of Prehistoric Australia and Its People, 2.

21 **Professor Richard Fullagar:** BA (Melb.) & PhD (La Trobe) (Centre of Archaeological Science/ School of Earth & Environmental Sciences - University of Wollongong) an archaeologist and Research Fellow with specialisations in stone tools and their usage, grinding stones and the migrations of Homo sapiens.

22 **David M. Price:** (School of Earth & Environmental Sciences - University of Wollongong) operated the very first luminescence laboratory in Australia (ANU), leading technician in Thermo luminescence dating - his 'Australian Slide Method' has become the worldwide standard.

23 **Professor Lesley Head:** (Previously University of Wollongong & Currently University of Melbourne) Geographer and ARC Laureate Fellow.

24 Richard Fullagar, David Price, and Lesley Head, "Early Human Occupation of Northern Australia: Archaeology and Thermoluminescence Dating of Jinmium Rock Shelter, Northern Territory," Top 100 Citations 70 (December 1, 1996): 751–73, https://doi.org/10.1017/S0003598X00084040.
25 Flood, Archaeology of the Dreamtime: The Story of Prehistoric Australia and Its People, 3.
26 Flood, 3 Cites: Bert Roberts, Richard Fullagar et el, May 1998. "Nature", May, vol. 393, pp 358-362.
27 Flood, 3 Cites: Bert Roberts, Richard Fullagar et el, May 1998. "Nature", May, vol. 393, pp 358-362.
28 Flood, 3.

29 **WLH 1: (Willandra Lakes Human 1) aka Mungo Women** A gracile female skeleton found at Lake Mungo, discovered in 1969 by Jim Bowler and dated between 24,710 to 26,000 years.

30 **WLH 3: (Willandra Lakes Human 3) aka Mungo Man** A gracile male skeleton found at Lake Mungo, discovered in 1974 by Jim Bowler, dated between 61,000 to 69,000 years. The body was covered in red ochre as a component of a sophisticated burial practice. There is some controversy around the date of this skeleton.

31 Rueparadis, Figure 40: Lake Mungo, June 21, 2018, Photograph, June 21, 2018, Own work, https://commons.wikimedia.org/wiki/File:Lake_Mungo_lunette.jpg (Rights: Creative Commons Attribution-Share Alike 4.0 International).

32 **WLH 50: (Willandra Lakes Human 50)** a robust male partial cranium/skullcap that was discovered in 1982, found at Lake Mungo by Alan Thorne, dated between 29,000 to 40,000 years.

33 Flood, Archaeology of the Dreamtime: The Story of Prehistoric Australia and Its People, 69.
34 Flood, 69.
35 Flood, 69
36 Flood, 69.
37 Flood, 69.
38 Flood, 69.
39 Flood, 69.
40 Flood, 69.
41 Darren Curnoe, Figure 41: WLH 50 Skullcap, January 20, 2011, January 20, 2011, https://doi.org/10.4061/2011/632484, https://commons.wikimedia.org/wiki/File:Willandra_Lakes_Human_50_calvaria.png (Rights: Creative Commons Attribution 3.0 Unported).
42 Flood, Archaeology of the Dreamtime: The Story of Prehistoric Australia and Its People, 69.
43 Flood, 69.
44 Flood, 69.
45 Flood, 69.

46 **Professor Alan Thorne:** He was one of Australia's leading academics (Archaeology, Biology, Human Anatomy) from A.N.U. (Australian National University). Alan Thorne has been extensively involved in numerous discoveries at Lake Mungo and Kow Swamp. He co-wrote a paper on W.L.H.3., suggesting the male individual carried a unique genetic strain that calls into question the "Out of Africa" theory. He was a leading proponent of Multiregional Hypothesis of Evolution Theory/ Regional Continuity Theory (see below*).
*__Multiregional Hypothesis of Evolution Theory/ Regional Continuity Theory:__ that Homo Erectus evolved into Homo sapiens in different locations around the world at about the same time. This theory was developed by Alan Thorne, Milford H. Wolpoff and Zinhu Wu.

47 Flood, Archaeology of the Dreamtime: The Story of Prehistoric Australia and Its People, 69–70.
48 Flood, 70.
49 James Maurice Bowler, Figure 42: Mungo Man, Unknown, Photograph, Unknown, sent by James Maurice Bowler, https://commons.wikimedia.org/wiki/File:Mungo_Man.jpg (Rights: Creative Commons Attribution-Share Alike 3.0).

50 **Professor Chris Stringer:** British physical anthropologist noted for his work on human evolution. Research Leader - Human Evolution with expertise in Human origins and Palaeoanthropology at the Natural History Museum. See: https://www.nhm.ac.uk/our-science/departments-and-staff/staff-directory/chris-stringer.html

51 Chris Stringer, "A Metrical Study of WLH-50 Calvaria," Journal of Human Evolution 34 (1998): 332.
52 Flood, Archaeology of the Dreamtime: The Story of Prehistoric Australia and Its People, 61.
53 Flood, 61.
54 Ryan Somma, Figure 43: Kow Swamp 1, January 1, 1980, Photograph, January 1, 1980, Homo Sapiens 13,000 to 9,000 Years Old, https://commons.wikimedia.org/wiki/File:Kow_Swamp1-Homo_sapiens.jpg (Rights: Creative Commons Attribution-Share Alike 2.0 Generic).
55 Flood, Archaeology of the Dreamtime: The Story of Prehistoric Australia and Its People, 61.

56 The Sydney Morning Herald, "The Bone Keeper's Dilemma," The Sydney Morning Herald, June 9, 2003, https://www.smh.com.au/world/the-bone-keepers-dilemma-20030609-gdgwg2.html.
57 Morning Herald.

58 **Professor Robert Foley:** of Cambridge University, Research Fellow with specialisations in Palaeoanthropology, Human Evolution and Behavioural Ecology.

59 Morning Herald, "The Bone Keeper's Dilemma."
60 Flood, Archaeology of the Dreamtime: The Story of Prehistoric Australia and Its People, 63.

61 **Yowie:** An Australian name for unidentified hominid/biped, its potential habitat being somewhere within the remote wilderness. They could be classified as a Hominid Cryptid. Two types are talked about a large variety 6-15ft and a smaller one 4-5ft. Described as hairy and ape-like, with large feet, behaviour ranges from shy to aggressive and there is a long history of sightings from the late 1700's by the British Colonial settlers into the present and is mentioned within the Australian Original Folklore too. Equivalent entities of the yowie are found throughout the whole globe, including the Yeti (Himalayas), Yeren (China), Sasquatch/Bigfoot (North America), Tjutjuna/Chuchunaa (Russia-Siberia), Red Headband (Comoros), Orang Mawas (Malaysia), Nguoi Rung (Vietnam), Hibagon or Hinagon (Japan), Am Fear Liath Mòr (Scotland), Wudewas/Wood Men (British Isles), Brenin Llwyd (Wales), Barmanou (Afghanistan/ Pakistan) and Almas (Mongolia, Central Asia, Caucasus).

62 Slater, Scribes of the Stone Age, 30.
63 Slater, 32.

64 **Dr. Hermann Klaatsch:** (Professor) from Germany a physician, anatomist, physical anthropologist and writer. He travelled to Australia 1904 to 1907 was fascinated with Australian Original culture and remains. He helped separate the sciences from religion.

65 Professor / M.D. Hermann Klaatsch, The Evolution and Progress of Mankind, ed. Profosser / M.D. Adolf Heilborn, trans. Joseph McCabe (New York, NY: Frederick A. Stokes Company Publishers, 1923), 136–37.
66 Klaatsch, 137.
67 Klaatsch, 136.
68 Professor / M.D. Hermann Klaatsch, Figure 44: Professor / M.D. Hermann Klaatsch, 1923, Photograph, 1923, 5. From: Professor / M.D. Hermann Klaatsch, The Evolution and Progress of Mankind, ed. Professor / M.D. Adolf Heilborn, trans. Joseph McCabe (New York, NY: Frederick A. Stokes Company Publishers, 1923.
69 Klaatsch, The Evolution and Progress of Mankind, 136.
70 Robert Lawlor, Voices of the First Day: Awakening in the Aboriginal Dreamtime (Rochester, Vermont: Inner Traditions International, 1991), 120–21.

71 **Githabul:** Australian Original Tribe (a part of the Bundalung*[sic] Language Confederation) and land estate in Northern N.S.W. and Queensland incorporating the area with the towns of Woodenbong and Urbenville.

72 Steven Strong, Karno W., and Frederic Slater, Figure 45: Possum Dreaming - Mix of Karno's & Slater's Symbols, 2013, 1939 2015, Diagram, 2013, 1939 2015 Compiled by Steven Strong.

Chapter 10: "Stone Age Authors"

1 Slater, Scribes of the Stone Age, 47–62.

Chapter 11: The Hows, Whys, Who and Where

1 **Murree Gwalda:** Eliza Hamilton Dunlop's First Language dictionary also the soul/spirit language which brings forth to the earth of the light of God.

2 Karno W., Sothern Law Confederation, 2014.
3 Dellene Strong, Figure 46: Southern Law Confederation Map, 2023, Diagram, 2023 Map Template: by User:Golbez, 2006. "Blank map of the territory governed by the states of Australia", https://commons.wikimedia.org/wiki/File:Australia_states_blank.png (Rights: GNU Free Documentation License, Creative Commons Attribution-Share Alike 3.0 Unported & Creative Commons Attribution 2.5 Generic).
4 Karno W., More DNA, 2014.

5 **Southern Law Confederation:** "Ramindjeri spokesperson Karno (dec. surname withheld) has spoken on many occasions in some detail about the Southern Law network that has been in existence for hundreds of thousands of years. According to Karno this web of tribes runs 300 miles inland from the coast, beginning up near the Kimberleys (W.A.), the area of influence extends all around the Australian coastline down to South Australia, Victoria and all the way up the east coast until reaching Cape York. By landmass it would make up about one quarter of the Australian continent, and by Old Way sensibilities and norms it is still in existence and will continue functioning as a binding agent for all tribal estates under its jurisdiction." Steven Strong, Evan Strong, and Karno (Surame with held), "From the Beginning with Karno (Surname Withheld) Ramindjeri Spokesperson," 2014, http://forgottenorigin.com/from-the-beginning-article-by-steven-evan-strong-with-karno-walker-ramindjeri-spokesperson

6 W., Sothern Law Confederation.

7 **Reverend William Ridley:** (1819-1879) English born Linguist, classics Professor, journalist, theological tutor and Presbyterian minister with a particular interest in the Gumilaroi/Kamilaroi Original Language.

8 **Robert Hamilton Matthews:** (1841-1918) aka "Birrarak" a surveyor, magistrate, coroner and anthropologist, member of Royal Society of New South Wales & Anthropological Institute of London/ Royal Anthropological Institute who studied the Original Australians. Published 171 anthropological works notably on kinship and marriage rules and customs, male initiation, mythology and linguistics. He was regarded well by Original people and overseas contemporaries, but was isolated, unsupported and maligned within Australia amongst the anthropology community at that time. However, in more recent times his works, contributions and legacy are now considered an important resource.

9 Slater, Scribes of the Stone Age, 48.
10 Slater, 48.
11 Author Unknown, Figure 47: R. H. Mathews, 1909, Photograph, 1909, [1], https://commons.wikimedia.org/wiki/File:R_H_Mathews.jpg (Rights: Public Domain).
12 Slater, Scribes of the Stone Age, 52.
13 Slater, 52.
14 Slater and Patterson, ed., Personal Letters - Correspondences - Notes no. 2.
15 Slater and Patterson, ed. no. 2.
16 Slater and Patterson, ed. no. 1.
17 Slater and Patterson, ed. no. 2.
18 Slater and Patterson, ed. no. 3.
19 Slater and Patterson, ed. no. 6.
20 Slater and Patterson, ed. no. 2.
21 Goddard and Slater, "Burragurru or Devil's Rock: An Aboriginal Burial Ground in the Wollombi District [Manuscript]. - Trove," 14.
22 Goddard and Slater, 14.
23 Slater and Patterson, ed., Personal Letters - Correspondences - Notes no. 2 & 6.
24 Slater and Patterson, ed. no. 2.
25 Goddard and Slater, "Burragurru or Devil's Rock: An Aboriginal Burial Ground in the Wollombi District [Manuscript]. - Trove," 14.
26 Slater and Patterson, ed., Personal Letters - Correspondences - Notes no. 6.
27 Slater, Scribes of the Stone Age, 50.
28 Slater, 50.
29 Slater, 60.
30 Slater, 6.
31 Slater, 6.
32 Slater, 52.
33 Smiling Pixell, Figure 48: Great Record Book, 2016, Picture, 2016, https://pixabay.com/photos/hand-fire-rosetta-stone-fingers-1393606/ (Rights: Pixabay License).

Chapter 12: Finding Nemo

1 Taken, Figure 49: Nemo, 2014, Photograph, 2014, https://pixabay.com/photos/clownfish-anemonefish-fish-sea-426567/ (Rights: Pixabay License).
2 Slater and Patterson, ed., Personal Letters - Correspondences - Notes no. 6.
3 Slater, Scribes of the Stone Age, 6.
4 Slater, 6.
5 W., More DNA.
6 Slater, Scribes of the Stone Age, 60.
7 Author Unknown, Figure 50: Rosetta Stone, 2009, Picture, 2009, https://commons.wikimedia.org/wiki/File:Rosetta_Stone_BW.jpeg (Rights: Public Domain).

8 **Rosetta Stone:** a stele (slab that is taller than wide, either fashioned in stone or wood) of granodiorite (like granite) of decrees (three versions - Ancient Egyptian hieroglyphics demotic script {Nile Delta} and Ancient Greek) from 196 BC on behalf of King Ptolemy V Epiphanes. The significance being the Rosetta Stone was the key to deciphering the ancient Egyptian Scripts.

9 Deselect 99designs, Figure 51: Blue Kachina Star Prophecy, 2018, Picture, 2018, https://pixabay.com/photos/wallpaper-space-desktop-universe-3584226/ (Rights: Pixabay License).

10 **Hopi:** a Native American sovereign nation located primarily in north-eastern Arizona USA. The Hopi have retained a lot of their cultural identity and are organised into matrilineal clans. They have a complex mythological/religious system notably are custodians of prophecies that details a time of purification, upheaval and then peace.

11 **Blue Star Kachina Prophecy:** an ancient prophecy that describes the coming the coming of a new world heralded by the Blue Star Kachina*(see below). Specifically - the Star People and their wisdom/knowledge will return again, and that the world progresses through cycles which are separated by cataclysms. We are currently living in the end stage of Fourth World and the appearance of the Blue Star Kachina will bring about the change-over into the Fifth world. There are parallels to other culture prophecies on this too e.g. Mayan, Planet X, the myth of Quetzalcoatl and the Horned Serpent. Apparently 8 out of the 9 Signs of Destruction have already been fulfilled. See More at - [https://psy-minds.com/hopi-kachina-prophecy/]
*derator**Kachinas:** are beings from above (a high western mountain) who inhabit humans from solstices every year and act as guardian spirits.

12 Newcastle Sun, "Presented to Frederic Slater ... (Award)" (Newcastle Sun, March 29, 1924).

Chapter 13: Nobody Cared

1 Evan Strong, Figure 52: Frederic Slater's Award, 2023, Photograph, 2023.
2 Evan Strong, Figure 51: Frederic Slater's Award, 2023, Photograph, 2023 Engraving on Award Plaque.
3 Strong Engraving on Award Plaque.
4 Strong Engraving on Award Plaque.
5 Evan Strong, Figure 53: Close-up of Frederic Slater's Award, 2023, Photograph, 2023.
6 Strong, Figure 51: Frederic Slater's Award Engraving on Award Plaque.
7 Strong Engraving on Award Plaque.
8 Heung Soon, Figure 54: Book of Translations - More to Follow, 2019, Photograph, 2019, https://pixabay.com/photos/note-diary-phrases-record-book-4121949/ (Rights Pixabay License).

Chapter 14: Goddard's Report

1 Slater, Scribes of the Stone Age, 19–27.

Appendix 1:

1 No. 1 Patrick F. Cardinal Moran, "Discovery of Australia by de Quiros in the Year 1606" (A Project Gutenberg of Australia & The Australian Catholic Truth Society, 2006), 1–32, https://gutenberg.net.au/ebooks06/0600641h.html (Rights: http://gutenberg.net.au/licence.html).

Appendix 2:

1 Goddard and Slater, "Burragurru or Devil's Rock: An Aboriginal Burial Ground in the Wollombi District [Manuscript]. - Trove," 1–9.

Appendix 3:

1 Jon Wyatt, "Article," August 13, 2022.

About the Authors:

1 Samarah Wood, Figure 55: Evan & Steven Strong, 2016, Photograph, 2016.

Index

A

Akkadians 22, 34
Animism 34
ankh 45, 46
Anthropological Society 19, 26, 31
arra 71
Atlantis 11, 38
Aunty Beve 50
Aunty Minnie 49
Australian and New Zealand Science Conference 18
Australian Archaeological Educational and Research Society 17
Australian Museum 32

B

Baal 33
Babylon 40
Bahiame 76
Baiame 46, 47, 51, 52, 53
Bambara 48
Basedow 71
Belt of Orion 51
Between a Rock and a Hard Place 13
bina 71
Blaxland 90
Blue Kachinas 86
Blue Kachina Star Prophecy 86
Bolera-ngawl 76
Bolera-ngwal 76
Boobardy 51, 52, 53, 54
Book of Knowledge 42
Book of Searchings 34, 56
Book of Translations 33, 34, 56, 89
boomerang 71, 72
Bora 76
Bowler 61, 62
Brunswick Heads 12, 26
Bulgandry 50, 51, 54
Burragurra 18, 31, 42, 44, 45, 51, 53 54, 74, 75, 76, 86, 90, 92
Butherawuulay 76

C

Capertee 90
Cape York 78, 81
Carnegie Institute 20
Caumil 74
Caumil Murree 74
Chaldea 34

Collie 74
Colly 74
Cook 30
Cossack 60, 70
curriaree 59

D

Daramulum 46, 47
Debbil Debbil 42
De Quito 27, 28, 30
Devil's Rock 42, 90, 91
Dinna-yaree 42
Dr. Albert Churchward 56
Dravidian 72
Druid 58
Dunlop 20, 21, 22, 23, 26, 39, 44, 74, 76, 77, 79, 82
Duramulum 53, 76

E

Egyptian Book of the Dead 22, 34, 40
Elizabethan Age 57
Elkin 17, 55
Enright 19, 26, 42, 75

F

Flood 63, 64, 67
Foley 69
Fordham 19, 20, 26, 79
Fordwich 90
Fullagar 64

G

Gayrage 76
Ghungaw 57
Githubal 73
Gnostic 54
Goddard 19, 26, 31, 39, 42, 43, 45, 51
God of Inheritance 46, 47
Gosford 45, 55, 74, 75
gracile 65, 70
Great Barrier Reef 60, 62
Great Record Book 10, 11, 36, 39, 40, 41, 44, 79, 83
Greece 34, 40
Greenwell 19, 26
Gumilaroi 74, 75, 81

H

Hawkesbury 35, 42
Herodotus 34
Hopi 86
Horus 33
Howe's Mount 90
Hunter River 35

I

Isis 46

J

Java Man 68
jepar 71
Jinmium 60, 64
John Head 67
Julius Caesar 58
Jupiter 33

K

Kamil 74
kapata 71
Karaji 76
Karia 76
Kariong 48
Karno 13, 14, 15, 73, 78, 85
katabul 42
Kimberleys 54, 78
Klaatsch 71, 72
Kolle 74
Kon-fu-tse 22, 34, 40
Kow Swamp 60, 68, 69, 70
Kumbakuluku 35

L

Lake Condah 30
Lake George 60, 62, 63
Lake Mungo 60, 65, 68
larra 71
Lemuria 11
Lesley Head 64
little people 70
Loki 34

M

Macdonald River 35, 92
manda 71
Maroota 31
matta 59
Matthews 75, 79
mera 71
Milky Way 50
Mirriwulla 76
Mogo Creek 90
Moran 27, 28, 32
Mount Irvine 91
Mount Murwin 90
Mount Werong 90
Mount Wilson 91
Mount Yengo 52
Mu 36
Mulla Mulla 53
Mullumbimby 12, 26, 80
Mundowa 52, 53, 58, 59, 76
Murree Gwalda 27, 39, 74, 75, 77, 78, 79, 81, 82, 86
Muun 59, 76

N

Nameless One 52, 53
Namoi 74, 76
Nell of the Navy 25
Neolithic 34
Ngalbal 46
Ngutta Ngintabe your 52
Nilotic 33, 34
nulka-nulka 35
Numbardy 51, 52, 53

O

Odin 34
Ogam 58
Osiris 33, 46
Out-of-Africa theory 60, 62, 63, 64, 65, 70
Ouwendyke 62

P

Palaeolithic 34
Panaramitee 60, 63, 64
Parra 59
Parramatta 59
Parrawee 59
Petrie 56
Pharaohs of the Southern Land 23
Pharaohs of the South Land 37, 39
Philip III 27
Phoenicia 34
Plato 8
Pleistocene 69
Pleistocian 35
Point Ritchie 60, 61, 62
Port Curtis 27
Price 64

R

Radcliffe Brown 76
Ramindjeri 13, 73, 78
Richard Patterson 12
Ridley 74, 79
robust 66, 68
Rome 34, 40
Rosetta Stone 85, 86

S

Sahara 34
Science Congress 19, 26, 31, 51
Scribes of the Stone Age 10, 12, 21, 22, 24
Sea Foam and Passion Flowers 25
Shakespeare 57, 58
Shelley Beach 30
Singh 62, 63
Sky Heroes 10, 12, 17, 54
Solon 8
Southern Law Confederation 78
Squire 75
St. Albans 90
Standing Stones 12, 13, 14, 16, 17, 18, 19, 26, 73, 79, 80, 81
Stringer 68, 69
Sydney University 17, 18, 19, 31, 32, 55

T

taurai 52
Terra Nullius 38
The Pharaohs of the South Land 34
The Sins of the Fathers 25
Thoorale-moori 57
Thor 33, 34
Thorne 67, 70
Thoth 45, 50
Torres 29
Troy 24, 40
Turrawula ngai dhurudi 52
Turrawulla, Turrawulla, guiya ngaia kaoi 52
Tuwumba 71
Tyan Peak 90

W

Wa-booee 76
Wailwon 74
Walter Roche 57
Wandjina 54
warra 71
Whirl of the World 25
Whistler 39
Wiradhuri 74
WLH 1 65, 67, 68
WLH 3 65
WLH 50 66, 67, 68
Wollombi 19, 20, 35, 42, 44, 45, 53, 54, 55, 74, 76, 77, 79, 82
woomera 71
Wright 63
Wyatt 24, 88

Y

Yaldabaoth 54
Yaltaboath 54
Yango 74, 76, 90, 91, 92
Yango Creek 92
Yarraman 35
Young and Champillon 35
Yowies 70
Yugar ngutta 52

Z

Zeus 33

www.ingramcontent.com/pod-product-compliance
Lightning Source LLC
Chambersburg PA
CBHW051559010526
44118CB00023B/2758